A Retreat with St. Bonaventure

St. Bonaventure

A Retreat with
St. Bonaventure

Leonard J. Bowman

E L E M E N T
Rockport, Massachusetts • Shaftesbury, Dorset
Brisbane, Queensland

Published in the U.S.A. in 1993 by
Element, Inc.
42 Broadway, Rockport, MA 01966

Published in Great Britain in 1993 by
Element Books Limited
Longmead, Shaftesbury, Dorset

Published in Australia in 1993 by
Element Books Ltd for
Jacaranda Wiley Ltd
33 Park Road, Milton, Brisbane, 4064

Text design by Roger Lightfoot
Typeset by ROM-Data, Falmouth, Cornwall, England
Printed and bound in the U.S.A. by
Edwards Brothers, Inc.

British Library Cataloguing-in-Publication
Data available

Library of Congress Cataloging in Publication
Data available

ISBN 1–85230–289–5

To
Anne, Emily, Sarah and Claire

Sources of my interruptions and inspirations

Contents

Acknowledgments

Thanks to my wife Anne, to Kirk Scott-Craig and to Patrick Miner for their helpful comments on the manuscript, and to Patrick Miner and Felipe Tello for helping to remove the pesky locust tree described in chapter 3. Thanks to Richard Payne and the staff at Element, Inc., for guidance in bringing the book to its completion. Thanks also to the people of St. Joseph's Church, Rock Island, Illinois, for being a vital Christian community. And thanks to the people of Teikyo Marycrest University for being, from time to time, a learning community at its best.

Scripture texts used in this work, unless otherwise noted, are taken from the *New American Bible with Revised New Testament*, copyright ©1986 by the Confraternity of Christian Doctrine, 3211 Fourth Street, N.E., Washington, D.C. 20017–1194, and are used with permission. All rights reserved.

Scripture quotations marked "RSV" are from the Revised Standard Version of the Bible, copyright 1946, 1952, 1971 by the Division of Christian Education of the National Council of Churches of Christ in the USA, and used with permission.

Scripture quotations marked "JB" are from *The Jerusalem Bible*, copyright 1966 by Darton, Longman & Todd, Ltd. and Doubleday, a division of Bantam Doubleday Dell Publishing Group, Inc. Reprinted by permission.

Quotations from Bonaventure's *Itinerarium Mentis in Deum* and *Lignum Vitae* are taken from Ewert Cousins' translation published by Paulist Press in 1978 and used with permission; citations are in parentheses by chapter and section, e.g., (Prologue:3), or (4:2). References to Bonaventure's Latin *Opera Omnia* are from the Quarracchi edition.

Material from *The Documents of Vatican II: In a New and Definitive Translation With Commentaries and Notes by Catholic, Protestant and Orthodox Authorities*, edited by Walter M. Abbott, copyright 1966 by America Press, is reprinted by permission of the Crossroad Publishing Company.

GENERAL INTRODUCTION

One of the greatest spiritual classics of the Western world is *The Soul's Journey into God*, the *Itinerarium* written by St. Bonaventure in the year 1259. Almost as influential is his *Tree of Life*, a series of meditations based mainly on the Gospels. Bonaventure was a follower of Saint Francis of Assisi. He was Minister General of the Franciscan Order, one of the thirteenth century's most outstanding theologians, a cardinal of the Church, and a saint.

I am convinced that *The Soul's Journey* is worth following today as a spiritual ascent through experience and thought. Likewise *The Tree of Life* is worth climbing as a way of praying the Scriptures.

However, this conviction did not come easily for me. When as a graduate student I first read Bonaventure, I found him alien and confusing, even in translation. But as I continued to study his writings—and at the same time struggled along my own intellectual and spiritual journey—my appreciation for Bonaventure grew. I came to recognize him as an inspiring mentor and a challenging guide. Gradually he came alive for me, and now I dare to regard him as a friend.

In *A Retreat with St. Bonaventure*, I seek to bring the reader closer to my friend Bonaventure. I invite you to meet him from the perspective of a contemporary Catholic layperson in the hope that this may help you bridge the distance separating us from him, a distance in time and in ways of thinking and living.

In order to attempt this meeting, we have to make two risky assumptions: one about how we should relate to a medieval text and the other about our prayer-relation to a saint.

A Retreat with St. Bonaventure is based directly on two classic texts. But it is not just a commentary on those texts. I believe that through such a text we meet a person. If we talk with a friend, of course we attend to what is said. But even more important, we sense and respond to what is not directly said—feeling tones, sparks of joy or sadness, and at the deepest level that ambiguous mix of strength and frustration, insight and confusion, that marks the mystery of a person on the way toward God. If we succeed in catching the spirit of our friend, we can feel with him and anticipate how he would respond to a problem or question that *we* face.

This friend happens to be a canonized saint, and so our conversation with him might be called "prayer." Such prayer takes place within the communion of saints. That in turn occurs best in the Eucharist, when we are gathered side by side with the saints in quest of God and in praise of God. The saints are then beside us, and our prayer is *with* them toward God.

Distance is a problem. Bonaventure is a man of *his* time. I believe that if we catch his spirit through his writings, he can guide our way too—but in the terms of *our* time. We can let him respond to contemporary developments like the renewed sense of Church, of the lay mission and of global interdependence. We can chide him for his shortcomings, too.

But this conversation takes place within a larger community of sharing. Bonaventure himself is conversing with saints before him like Gregory of Nyssa, Augustine, Anselm and Francis. These in turn are responding to the Scripture. Then, as *we* converse with Bonaventure, still other persons join in: for me, Julian of Norwich, Nicholas of Cusa, Gerard Manley Hopkins, Martin Heidegger, John Macmurray, Wilfred Cantwell Smith, Huston Smith and Ewert Cousins, to name only a few. The word for this ongoing community of sharing is *tradition*. And this tradition is not composed just of texts and interpretations of texts: it is relationship upon relationship of persons.

There are two ways you may wish to use this book as a guide in your own reflection. You may simply use *A Retreat with St. Bonaventure* alone as a point of departure for meditation. It is intended as a series of contemporary reflections, broken down into numbered units, which respond to Bonaventure and which follow the pattern and spirit of his writings.

Or you may wish to converse more directly with Bonaventure himself. In that case, I recommend Ewert Cousins' translations of these writings published in 1978 in the Paulist Press Classics of Western Spirituality. I used that translation as a basis for this work, along with Bonaventure's Latin. If you choose this alternative, you will notice that Bonaventure's texts are divided into numbered units of thought. The unit numbers in *A Retreat with St. Bonaventure* directly correspond to Bonaventure's (except for chapter 8 of *The Soul's Journey*, for Bonaventure's work has only seven chapters). Sometimes my unit will present an interpretive response to the insight in the corresponding unit of Bonaventure, sometimes a twentieth-century reinterpretation, sometimes a departure or an alternative. I suggest then that you go back and forth, reading a unit of Bonaventure and then the corresponding unit of this book. That method will also let you share in my own struggle with these texts, and you may find that at least amusing.

You may want to pace your reflections in accord with the time you have available. For instance, a seven-day retreat would allow a person to reflect, during each of the first four days, on one two-chapter level of *The Soul's Journey*, and then take one four-branch part of *The Tree of Life* for each of the last three days. Or you may wish to read *The Soul's Journey* or *The Tree of Life* in a single sitting, and then reread it, or selected parts, more slowly.

Some basic information about St. Bonaventure will be helpful in your reflection.

St. Bonaventure was born probably in the year 1217 in the small town of Bagnoregio, in Tuscany about a hundred kilometers north of Rome. He was baptized John di Fidanza, named after his father, a physician for the town. While young John was growing up, Francis of Assisi was preaching in the towns of Italy and gathering followers into what was to become the Franciscan Order. (Francis died in 1226 and was canonized a saint two years later.) In 1236, when John was about nineteen years old, he went to study at the University of Paris, the intellectual center of Europe at the time. About six years later he entered the Franciscan Order, taking the name Bonaventura. Then he undertook advanced studies in theology. He was teaching Scripture by the year 1248 and theology by the year 1253. He was recognized as Master (the thirteenth-century equivalent of Distinguished Professor) in 1257. That same year he was elected Minister General of the Franciscan Order to succeed John of Parma, who had resigned in the midst of a serious controversy that threatened to split the Order. Bonaventure then struggled to hold the Order together by charting clear directions for its future and by keeping different points of view balanced (there were even some nasty charges of heresy in the wind).

In the year 1259, Bonaventure made a retreat on Mount Alverno (or La Verna). This was a mountain of steep cliffs topped by thick woods, the very spot where thirty-five years earlier St. Francis had been marked with the wounds of Christ while rapt in vision of a six-winged angel in the form of the crucified Christ. Bonaventure climbed the mountain in search of inspiration as he struggled to guide Francis's Order. One result of the retreat is *The Soul's Journey into God,* a meditation based partly on the six-winged Seraph (angel) of Francis's vision.

Bonaventure came back down the mountain with a lot of work to do. He preached through Italy and France, and he wrote voluminously. In 1260, he developed the first Constitution for the Franciscan Order. In 1261, he had to preside at the trial and censure of his predecessor and friend, John of Parma.

Meanwhile old tensions at the University of Paris grew into open conflict. Bonaventure had taught that all the fields of knowledge were interrelated as aspects of humanity's earthly journey back to God. But others insisted that the fields of knowledge should be independent of each other and autonomous. While there was merit to that view (Thomas Aquinas held it to an extent), Bonaventure argued that it could split faith from reason, creation from revelation, and nature from grace: ultimately that it would split the human person and disrupt humanity's return to God. Many of Bonaventure's writings reflect his deep concerns about this conflict.

In 1273, Bonaventure was consecrated a bishop and named a cardinal. He was part of the ecumenical Council of Lyons—and he died there at the Council on July 15, 1274.

For Bonaventure, the whole world and everything in it is caught up in the Trinity. The Trinity for him is a far cry from the number puzzle many twentieth-century Catholics memorized from a catechism. Rather, Trinity describes the dynamic life of God that overflows into the created world and that draws everything back to union with God. Everything begins with God as fountain-fullness, out of goodness overflowing first to perfect expression, the Word, and then through the Word exploding outward into a numberless variety of creatures. The Spirit that is the bond of Father and Word is also the power bringing all creatures back into union with God. Human persons find themselves in a world that comes forth from the power of God as its cause, reflects the wisdom of the Word in its rational order and its beauty, and finds its goodness in returning praise to God in the Spirit. For Bonaventure, then, everything is caught up in this dynamic movement. The whole point of human existence is to recognize the power, wisdom and goodness of God in all creation, and to be led back through all creatures to contemplative union with God. *The Soul's Journey* directly traces the path of that recognition and return.

God's revelation, then, is first in the Word. That Word is incarnate in Jesus, and expressed first in the book of creation. Sadly, sin has made humankind forgetful of the language of that book, so the book of Scripture has been given as a kind of dictionary to remind us of that language. Ultimately, revelation occurs when persons recognize God in and through his expressions and respond in wonder and love. *The Tree of Life* reflects that growing revelation in relation to selections from the Bible.

Bonaventure's writing style is meditative and poetic. At the same time, his writing is very condensed, relying on his readers' familiarity with Scripture, philosophic and theological concepts, and methods of argument current in his time. *A Retreat with St. Bonaventure* cannot assume such familiarity with Scripture, philosophy and theology, and so will be less condensed and more descriptive.

Bonaventure's writings are a tapestry of references to Scripture. Frequently his references are brief, a phrase or even just a word. He could count on his hearers' familiarity with the Scripture to fill out the reference. Scripture is woven into this book in imitation of Bonaventure, but not as richly as he could, nor as briefly. In some cases the same passages are used here as in the corresponding units of his works, but perhaps more extensively quoted. Sometimes Scripture passages different from Bonaventure's selection are used, but used in a manner inspired by him.

Numbers bear special significance for Bonaventure, and the two works touched in this book are structured according to his theology of numbers. *Seven* is a number of completeness, reflecting the six days of creation in Genesis arriving at earthly fullness plus the seventh day of heavenly rest. Twelve is also a number of completeness, reflected in the twelve tribes of Israel and the twelve apostles. Both seven and twelve are made up of *three* and *four*. Three is the number of the Trinity, and the spiritual journey of return to God typically has three major levels. Four is the number of the directions and the seasons, the number of a complete turning. Both works, therefore, are designed to guide a person to fullness and to rest in God.

A Retreat with St. Bonaventure is therefore a double spiritual journey. First *The Soul's Journey* guides us through the world around us and then through the world within us into God above us. Then *The Tree of Life* guides us through the Gospel story to follow Christ in climbing the Cross and likewise in ascending into the heavenly kingdom.

ITINERARIUM

THE SOUL'S JOURNEY INTO GOD

The Stigmata of St. Francis

Introduction

Although *The Soul's Journey into God* was written in the year 1259, reading it and following its path does not have to be only a journey into the past. Rather, the follower can be faithful to the spirit of Bonaventure's original effort while working within the spiritual world of today.

There are limits to Bonaventure's journey. Bonaventure attempted to define a path for an intellectual to follow Francis. Hence it is an intellectual way that he maps—and that is its strength as well as its limit. This part of *A Retreat with St. Bonaventure* retains something of that limit and adds to it the limits (and strengths) of late twentieth-century American Catholic lay sensibility. Because of the Second Vatican Council, Church is given greater emphasis than in Bonaventure's theology; likewise, the distinctly secular character of the lay vocation is taken seriously. Further, philosophy is based less in abstract principles and more in descriptive experience connected with practical living in family and in community.

The main structural pattern of *The Soul's Journey* is the six-winged Seraph of Francis's vision. The vision is described as the crucified Christ with two wings outspread upward, two spread outward at the side, and the lower two folded over the body. Bonaventure, a lover of symbolic numbers, saw in the wings of the Seraph a pattern of three levels, with two aspects to each level. The first level, below ourselves, is the physical world and our perception of it. Next, within ourselves, is the soul, seen in the workings of reason and intellect and then in the workings of grace. Finally, above ourselves, is the reality of God recognized first as One and then as Trinity. This pattern of six connects automatically for Bonaventure with the six days of creation described in Genesis, followed by the seventh day of rest, where *The Soul's Journey* ends.

Four patterns of imagery also structure *The Soul's Journey*. First is the obvious image of *journey*. But this image is puzzling, for the journey does not go from one place to another. Several other motifs combine to give shape to this paradoxical journey. There is a path with a gate and a destination (Christ is each and all of these). But the journey is primarily an ascent: the climbing of a mountain, the mounting of a ladder. At the same time it is an inward journey, like exploring the cave of the inner self.

The motif of the inward journey links to a second image: the *Jerusalem Temple.* The journey begins in the outer court of the temple where the common people would gather for hymns and prayers during a festival. Then it moves within into the sanctuary where the priestly class was admitted for the ritual sacrifices at the altar, which stood at the base of a steep set of stone steps leading to the heavy curtain that closed off the Most Holy Place. Finally, the journey climbs to the Most Holy Place, a cube-shaped window-less room that was entered only by the high priest once a year on the Day of Atonement. At the center of this room stood the Ark of the Covenant, flanked by two huge carved winged beasts called Cherubim. The wings of the Cherubim were extended, the outer wing-tips just touching the walls, and the inner tips meeting some distance over the Ark. The empty circle formed over the Ark by the wings was called the Mercy Seat—the seat of God, the place where the invisible God was specially present among his people.

A third image, linked to the Temple image, is the kind of *light* that guides the journey. The light of the outer court is the light of common day. Once the journey enters the sanctuary, the light is that of the ritual lamps that line the sides of that space. But inside the Most Holy Place, the only light is God himself, physically indistinguishable from darkness.

A Retreat with St. Bonaventure tries to follow all these image patterns to an extent, but in a way adapted to a twentieth-century sensibility that is not attuned as Bonaventure was, for instance, to symbolic numbers.

Finally, the text of the *Itinerarium* is divided into chapters and numbered sections. Each numbered section contains a unit of insight developing that stage of the journey. This book also uses numbered sections and attempts a section-by-section correspondence with Bonaventure's text. Sometimes this writing will present an interpretive translation of the insight in the corresponding section of Bonaventure; sometimes a twentieth-century reinterpretation of that insight; sometimes a departure or an alternative. (Of course that correspondence does not apply to chapter 8, for Bonaventure's work has only seven chapters.) The reader using this book for a personal retreat may want to use the numbered sections as units of reflection.

The Soul's Journey begins with a prologue and then climbs

through six steps to rest in the presence of God. *A Retreat with St. Bonaventure* follows that structure with one addition: an eighth chapter that brings the journey back into the everyday responsibilities of life in the world.

Prologue

1. In the beginning
I call upon the First Beginning . . .

So Bonaventure began the work for which he is best known, *The Soul's Journey into God.*[1]

How are we to begin? Our own time seems remote from Bonaventure's age of faith. Our world is like an overplowed, eroded plain compared to the wild, beautiful heights of Mount Alverno where Bonaventure reflected, there in the very spot where St. Francis of Assisi was sealed by the marks of Christ's wounds.

Really, *can* we today follow Bonaventure's path into the presence of God? We have to try—if there is any hope for us.

And so in this beginning we too dare to call upon the presence of God hidden within *our* time and our world. Our call lacks the bold rhythm of Bonaventure's; he is after all a saint. But who is to say that the spiritual pinnacle of Bonaventure's time is more *real* after all than the windswept plain of today?

In the beginning—are we now called to *discover* that hidden presence of God, as it is to appear specially for our time? In our deprivation, are we called to rediscover God from whom comes every good and perfect gift?

The gift of Peace! "Then the peace of God that surpasses all understanding will guard your hearts and minds in Christ Jesus" (Phil. 4:7). Peace is a spiritual condition, a power within that *makes* peace, that is peaceable even with those who treat all human relationships as contest and conflict. How far we are from such peace, and how desperately it is needed in our time! Brother Bonaventure, is there hope for us?

2. Bonaventure too felt the *lack* of such peace! He too hungrily sought it! Yes, then, there is hope—that we who are without peace can come to the peace of God's presence and power. For us, too, there may be a path!

In the year 1259, burdened with the responsibilities of leading the young Franciscan Order, Bonaventure sought peace by returning to Mount Alverno. For the Order it was a time of turbulence, conflict and uncertainty. For the people of Bonaventure's world it was a time of upheaval, threat and foreboding. (In fact, many believed that Apocalypse would strike and the world would end in the next year, 1260.) Bonaventure came to that holy place hoping to discover a path for his time, for he already felt remote from the time of St. Francis. Francis had been a free spirit, able to soar above the entanglements and institutional structures where most of us have to live. Bonaventure faced the awesome challenge of translating the way of Francis into institutional patterns without stifling its spirit.

You see, Bonaventure was a priest, a professor, a leading philosopher and theologian of his day. But Francis had held himself back from the priesthood. Francis even saw book-learning as a spiritual danger. ". . . I admonish and exhort the brothers in the Lord Jesus Christ that they beware of all pride, vainglory, . . . cares and worries of this world," he had said in the Rule of the Order. "And those who are illiterate should not be eager to learn. Instead let them pursue what they must desire above all things: to have the Spirit of the Lord and His holy manner of working. . . ."[2]

When Bonaventure climbed Alverno in his search for peace, he didn't *know* he was a saint! He probably felt worried and confused. There he was, charged with guiding the heritage of St. Francis. Yet by necessity he was ensnarled in the cares and worries of his world, and by his own personal vocation he was committed to the pursuit of learning. Was there a path for him in his time, so different already, to follow the simple Francis into union with Christ? Father Francis, in this holy place where you met the Crucified, show us a way!

It is now seven hundred and thirty years since Bonaventure sought his way by returning to Alverno. This writer is a layperson, husband, father of three daughters in their teens, and a teacher at a small college. I write in a small room of an ordinary old house in an ordinary city that overlooks the Mississippi River in a very secular United States of America. Lacking the resources to travel to Alverno, I can return to the mind of Bonaventure through the classic text which he has left us, *The Soul's Journey into God.* Lacking the opportunity to withdraw for a time of quiet, I catch what moments I can of reflection, and hope that even in the interruptions—perhaps *especially* in the interruptions!—there may be revealed a special road into God for our time. And so, guided by Bonaventure's insight into Francis's vision of Christ, can we find a road within this ordinary, secular place toward the spiritual height?

But how can it be that a path like Bonaventure's can be found in the life of a layperson who is immersed in class schedules and ringing telephones and sick children and misbehaving automobiles? Shouldn't I at least arrange for a week or so of retreat in some sort of monastery?

That would be sensible. After all, we do need to step back from the pressures of life to regain perspective and to recharge our spirit.

But there is a risk. If we must *withdraw* from our ordinary life, will we really find a spiritual road for a contemporary layperson? Are we laity doomed, for a spiritual life, to have to escape our own lives and sneak off to be imitation monks for a while? Is God so absent from the actual life of a contemporary layperson that no way into God is to be found right within it?

I cannot believe so—for I believe that God has taken our actual life to himself by becoming fully human in Jesus.

So, while a special time of retreat is indeed desirable, it should not be necessary. Let us begin exactly where we find ourselves.

3. Bonaventure shows us that there are steps, phases, aspects of illumination by which a spiritual road will be revealed among the shadows of our lives. That means that a journey into God will be a process of growth and development. The way will become visible only in glimpses, flashes, a bit at a time. We need to be patient.

That means also that there are *different* aspects to the spiritual journey, perhaps even different routes for different people. It is one journey into God, yet a variety of ways within it. These ways begin from creatures and lead up into God. "Creatures" means everything that we are and that we experience in our ordinary lives. If Bonaventure's vision still holds true, then everything in our ordinary lives—*Everything!*—should open upward to reveal the presence of God; *Everything* should lead back into God.

But everything seems so closed and opaque, tearing us away from God. How are the details of our lives to open up? How are they to lead us back into God? How?

The door that opens up and the path that leads back, Bonaventure says, is Christ crucified. Of course! and we nod to the crucifix.

No, the *real* Christ crucified, who sent Paul tumbling and scrambling beside the road to Damascus and who set him to stuttering incoherently, "I have been crucified with Christ; yet I live, no longer I, but Christ lives in me . . ." (Gal. 2:19, 20, from the Greek). Christ who set Francis in such a state that the marks of nails and lance were burned into him!

How are we to pass through such a door! Must we encounter Christ so dramatically at the outset? Then what hope is there?

We can desire. We can hope, even beg. "In the same way, the Spirit too comes to the aid of our weakness; for we do not know how to pray as we ought, but the Spirit itself intercedes with inexpressible groanings" (Rom. 8:26).

Does that work today too? Does the Spirit work amid word processors and telephones? If the Lord of history is Lord of our time too, then the Spirit must work today and in today's terms.

How?

In seeking our way, we have to realize constantly that we *don't* yet really know Christ crucified, and we have to realize constantly that he is the one we seek. Then Paul, and Francis, will tell us that Christ has a way of showing up suddenly . . . in his own time, on his own terms within our time. We can desire. We can hope. We can beg. Stumbling and scrambling, we can start out on our quest. Perhaps there will be flashes of insight along the way.

4. Prayer. Our yearning, hoping and begging are prayer, even—especially?—when they are wordless. We can proceed with confidence, but only because it is God who draws us and Christ—yes, the Crucified—who can take up our spiritual ambiguity and somehow make Easter happen.

But do not proceed out of curiosity. One thing I have learned from years of studying the works of Bonaventure: one does not "do" Bonaventure study as one "does" accounting or even literary criticism. Even to begin to be fair to him, one has to give oneself to him. One has to be committed to spiritual quest and struggle. One has to be willing to let go and to be caught up in the wonder and power of his vision.

Be ready then, at least in what moments you can find or make, to slow down, to step back and to savor what is really happening within and around you. Try to find or build within your mind a little place of quiet where you can retreat, if only for seconds at a time.

But whatever we attempt gets nowhere unless it is God who acts in our efforts. We undertake something beyond what is possible for us on our own. Therefore be ready to subject everything to questioning, and be ready to be changed.

We set out on a journey, away from our habitual ways of thinking. But might it really be a journey home?

5. It seemed good to Bonaventure to write seven chapters. An eighth chapter is unwritten, but expressed in the struggle, work and anguish toward which Bonaventure set his face as he

descended from Alverno into the cares and worries that filled his own life's journey.

This writing tries to follow the path Bonaventure marked, but as a twentieth-century layperson. Do not let the limitations of this writer's life and spirit hinder your own quest. In whatever reflective moments you are able to find or make, seek to gather your awareness of your own life's flow. Then test what is suggested here: see how it resonates within the tones and rhythms of what God has given especially to you. Try to glean for yourself whatever you can from the richness of Bonaventure and Francis. Then perhaps there will be flashes and glimpses along the way that illuminate for you a path into God.

Here begins the reflection of the poor man in the desert.

Earth

This chapter will reflect on the various steps
of the journey into God, and then will begin that journey
by seeking out the hidden presence of God
left like footprints upon the visible world around us.

1. Happiness—is that what it is all for? To be happy in heaven forever, we were told as children. Meanwhile, the *pursuit* of happiness is sacred even to a secular nation.

And how does one pursue happiness? A typical trap is to think, "if only I had [fill in the blank], then I would be happy." And the blank can be filled with things like "more money," "more and better sex," "better health," "the respect I deserve!" and even "a better prayer life." Someone who so self-consciously pursues happiness is likely to return with tales of disappointment or with recognizable delusions. Happiness is not something one achieves by working for it.

It is better to be busy caring for others than to be worried about whether or not we are happy. Sometimes into such busy lives there do come moments of joy, flashes of recognition which flush a person's being and bring a momentary shudder. Then the moments pass and are gone, except perhaps for a lingering glow.

Such moments come by surprise. They come when the *I* that pursues happiness is left behind, at least for the moment. And that does not happen through effort. That comes as a gift, a grace.

But even while we thrash about, entangled within our busy selves, we can still hope and yearn and beg. Prayer again, wordless prayer. Such prayer, Bonaventure says, is the mother and wellspring of the upward flight of the soul toward mystical ecstasy. Yes, that very yearning that we *think* proves how *far* our ordinary lives are from holiness! Such prayer is the beginning of the journey.

> Lead me, Lord, in the path toward you,
> and you will bring me to know you;
> fill my heart with joy,

that I may recognize—My God!—who you are.
(Ps. 86:11, adapted from Bonaventure's Latin)

2. Can we take that yearning within us and accept it, not as a cry of frustration, but as the call of God to us? We can try! If we pray in this way, there may come flashes and glimpses of light. Right there in the whirl of what is happening within and around us, a path may appear that leads upward into God.

Of course we are remote from God! If we expect to find God — Zap! — right before us, of course we will feel frustrated and lost. We should start more modestly with what is closest to our ordinary, everyday consciousness. For if Bonaventure is right, shouldn't *everything* somehow open upward to reveal the presence of God?

So first we can try to appreciate the simple, natural things around us. Then perhaps they will become luminous and transparent, revealing bit by bit the hidden presence of God. After that, we may be ready to discover the mystery of persons—ourselves and those with whom we live and work. After all, that yearning call of God is there within every person. The destiny and adventure of the journey is there as well. Only after we can recognize God in and through what is close to us may we tentatively search, shading our eyes, toward that hidden reality itself into which our yearning reaches— God himself!

3. As these mysteries of world, persons and God start to open to us, then other things that we have heard may make sense in a new way. We may begin to understand what it meant for the people of Israel to emerge from slavery in Egypt, to wander through the wilderness, and to arrive at the mountain of God. We may delight in the daily rhythm of light that passes from gray to gold to blinding brightness and then back again. Gradually our appreciation of things and persons will reach beneath the surface to the heart, reach beyond the moment to timeless destiny. We may even discover God's hidden design at work:

> . . . a plan for the fullness of times,
> to sum up all things in Christ, in heaven and on earth.
> (Eph. 1:10)

But other mysteries may open up as well, mysteries undreamed of by Bonaventure himself. For in this threefold path—through the visible world, through persons, and into ultimate mystery—Bonaventure has summarized the principal spiritual ways of all the world's religious traditions. Therefore, as we travel this path, we may suddenly understand the landscape painting of a Chinese Taoist sage. The simple Japanese tea ceremony may bring a flash of recognition. We may discover a traveling companion in the Buddhist following the Eightfold Path. Perhaps we will sense what *Atman* means to the Hindu. And even be struck speechless by the power of the simple proclamation of Islam, "There is no God but God"; nothing matters but God.

4. These ways are very natural, in the sense that they arise from and embrace the ordinary world within which we live. For Bonaventure, everything that exists is touched by grace. Everything within us and around us is from God, reflects God, and is called to God. Salvation is not just for the soul. It is for the whole being and for the world as well.

Whenever we act or think, the many levels of our being move together all at once. Notice what happens if I merely glance out the window at a tree. My body moves so that my eyes focus on the tree, and I perceive it. I then recognize it within my mind as a tree and respond at least vaguely with joy or disappointment. Deep within that joy or disappointment there is a reaching and a yearning beyond. All this is such a simple experience! In everything that we do, all the levels of our being are involved at once: physical, mental, sexual, emotional, spiritual, social, transcending. And everything, every level, can open toward God.

Is that part of what it means, that ancient command?

> Hear, O Israel: The Lord our God is one Lord; and you shall love the Lord your God with all your heart, and with all your soul, and with all your might. (Deut. 6:4–5, RSV)

Is that it? God is one; all God's creation is one; and we are to be at one in our journey of love into God? Bonaventure says that in this is perfect observance of the Law and full Christian wisdom as well.

5. As we try to travel this way that is three ways and, as we will see, even six ways, we may recognize suddenly that now the stories and the symbols of the Bible have new meaning for us. They are no longer something outside of us, but we can enter within them and they within us. (Yes, if we want to undertake this journey, we must try to know and love the Bible as Bonaventure did.)

The path we follow echoes the rise of creation in the first verses of the book of Genesis: six days in which God created realities ever closer to himself, and a seventh day of rest when yearning is fulfilled and there is real rest. With Solomon we may find ourselves climbing step by step the throne of wisdom, and discover for ourselves:

> Receive my instruction in preference to silver,
> and knowledge rather than choice gold.
> For Wisdom is better than corals,

and no choice possession can compare with her.
(Prov. 8:10–11)

With Isaiah we may feel worthless before God, and with eager terror we may sense God transforming us in the spinning, burning power of the Seraphim. (In such a Seraph the Crucified came to Francis on Mount Alverno and burned into him the marks of the cross.) Perhaps we will climb Sinai with Moses into the frightening, beckoning fire of God. Or with Peter and James and John suddenly have the ordinary realities around us transfigured, revealing the presence of—Jesus! my God!—that has been right here with us all along. Rise, and do not be afraid.

6. But if we want to undertake this journey, we will have to awaken dimensions of our mind and spirit that our culture does not usually nurture. We are schooled in composition and calculation, problem solving and cost accounting. But as we travel along Bonaventure's path, we must grow more sensitive to the currents and rhythms of our inner selves. We must appreciate more the realities beyond the practical. We must attune ourselves more to realities which are not for the day but are for all time, even timeless.

7. Quite a task! To rediscover the deeper dimensions of our world, of our inner selves, and of our images of God. But this too will come as a grace, bit by bit. After all, these dimensions are *there* within us and around us.

Or have they been lost or destroyed?

Have they remained asleep because we fear them and have run from them into our busyness? There is also the danger that we might misread the yearning within and imagine that by chasing after more money, sex, respectability, even prayer, we will satisfy that yearning. Ironically, such chasing leads us *away* from what we so deeply yearn for.

Perhaps the real point of spiritual effort is to learn that our effortful selves are empty! Am I saved? Am I in grace? Do I really know and understand? Are those questions really, ultimately, important?

> Suddenly a violent storm came up on the sea . . .
> They came and woke him, saying,
> "Lord, save us! We are perishing!"
> He said to them,
> "Why are you terrified, O you of little faith?"
> Then he got up, rebuked the winds and the sea,
> and there was a great calm.
> (Matt. 8:24–26)

Do not be anxious for yourselves; seek first the Kingdom (see Matt. 6:25–34). But how on earth does one do that?

Don't be discouraged; after all, isn't it God who acts, and the Spirit who teaches?

In whatever way we are given to let go of ourselves, gradually or once at a crash, as we let go we will be relieved of our tense ambitions and our tight defenses, making room for the surprise and the gift. It is God who acts, and we need to move our *selves* out of his way. The storms of anxiety and the clouds of uncertainty swirl around our need to feel secure in our *selves*, with our destiny under control. That need drives us toward tangible certainties, be they material, sensual, or busily religious. Unwittingly we may turn away from God even when we think we pursue him.

Let go; seek the Kingdom.

Bonaventure's journey is worth trying. As we take steps along this path, our desires should gradually shift away from self-satisfaction or self-justification. Understanding should begin to open. The tangible world around us should begin to be transparent. What we read and think should open upward. Our relationships should deepen. God beckons.

And it is our *whole being* in which God wishes to act. It is our *whole world* that Christ wishes to draw into reconciliation and transformation.

8. Are you serious about undertaking this journey? Then first let go of concern for yourself, even for your own spiritual state. Then pray—gather that inner yearning together with the flow of your own life. Let that prayer pass over into action so that your life comes to move with growing appreciation for the mystery of the world and the mystery of God's people. In what reflective moments you are able to find or make, seek out an inner place of quiet where you can step back from the rush, slow down and savor what is really happening within and around you. And leave yourself open for wordless moments of insight or joy. Gradually those reflective moments should grow in frequency and richness, the wordless moments in depth and intensity. Step by step, bit by bit we will be drawn, ascending the mountain of God.

9. Well, then, let us begin our journey! In order to begin, though, we first have to realize exactly where we stand. We stand at the *bottom* of the ladder. We stand among the Hebrew people still in slavery in Egypt, perhaps even with those who were angry at Moses for calling them to freedom (see Exod. 5:21). We stand among the disciples of Jesus who heard him, but "they did not realize what he was trying to tell them" (John 10:6).

For all that, we can at least try to stand *ready*—ready to be led back out of Egypt to the mountain of God, ready to pass over from slavery to freedom. Are we ready to pass from darkness to the "true light, which enlightens everyone" (John 1:9)?

But we start with the simple and ordinary things close to us. For if God created the world around us, then shouldn't obvious and immediate things somehow reveal the artist and craftsman who created them? One would think so. But how often do people in our society recognize the craftsman while looking at his works? (See Wisd. 13:1.) Have we forgotten how to praise?

> Let the heavens be glad and the earth rejoice;
>> let the sea and what fills it resound;
>>> let the plains be joyful and all that is in them!
> (Ps. 96:11–12)

Things close to us must become transparent, if we are going to make the transition from darkness to light and so transcend ourselves in the journey of transformation that we have started.

Let's take a closer look at those obvious and immediate things. Like detectives, we have to search out the telltale footprints that God has left upon his creation.

10. First we have to realize that we take a good deal for granted about the physical world around us. As I write these words, I glance out the window behind me to check the weather. In the gray light of early morning, I see snow swirling lightly around the dark bare branches of an ash tree, while cars swish down the shiny black street in the valley beyond. Simple things like these are there, forming a reliable world around us. Has it ever occurred to us that we should be astonished that they are there at all? Or even that they are there in a way which is at least a little beautiful?

Here we are, together with these things, in a moment of time. Others have been where we are, just as others have stood as I do looking out this very window in this ninety-year-old house. Others will come after us. We are caught up in the current of time. But how often have we paused to wonder at the kindly connectedness of its flow?

Outside my window the cars drive busily toward their destinations; the snow swirls to rest on the earth; the tree waits. At the same time all form a moment of beauty. There are so many dimensions and levels of the world around us! How can we learn to hear and appreciate its harmony and its destiny?

If we do not forget to be astonished and grateful and alert, perhaps we can come to recognize the power of God presenting the world to us, the wisdom of God sustaining it, the goodness of God in the overflow of beauty within these ordinary, practical things.

11. Let's try it. I am going to look again, more closely, at that ash tree. You may wish to spend some wordless moments just gazing at an object, preferably something growing naturally from the earth, like a tree (or a flower, if you are reading in a blooming season). Gaze at it, and let its simple presence fill your mind. Then explore your awareness to find whether you can see something like what I gradually glimpse as I gaze at the ash tree outside my winter window.

First, and obviously, it is *there*. But it is not there because I wanted it or imagined it. Unbidden, gratuitous, surprising (for it need not be at all, nor need I), it continues to stand there presenting itself to me, continuously emerging as a gift into my awareness. "Data," a scientist would say. Given. Can you sense the gift in what you gaze upon? Do you notice that our minds silently reach from this gift toward one who gives?

The dark branches of the ash tree sway in the bitter wind. Unlike the fine fingers of the elm and locust branches nearby, these branches jut thickly, all knobby, into the surrounding gray air. Small branches curve forth from larger with a bend like a bowl or a cup. One heavy branch reaches darkly toward my window, tilting the balance of the tree.

It is this specific, unique tree that encounters me, not a tree in general or even a typical ash tree. This tree—irreducible, irreplaceable—presenting itself to me in all the uniqueness of its thick, knobby, slightly unbalanced, very ordinary branches. This is true of every real thing that we see. There is nothing else exactly like it in the entire universe. As we gaze, the entire universe stops short here and rests, pausing in respect for the unique integrity of this particular being.

As I gaze, I sense half-consciously the white ridge that marks the lip of the little valley, beyond that the black street below, the white slope rising across, then gray sky and imaginable horizons. Likewise as you gaze, softly become conscious of the surrounding world.

So as we gaze upon a particular thing in its particular place and time, gradually we grow aware that we are here with it, here in an insignificant place that happens at the moment to be where the entire world comes to focus for us. We live in a world!—and everything surrounding that we see and that is beyond our eyesight embraces us in its gathering unity. Given. God, what a powerful thing to be a simple unbalanced ash tree caught up in the embrace of your universe!

Poets and artists know about the power of simple, ordinary

things. They labor and struggle to give us words or canvas, so that perhaps we will pause and pay attention—and perhaps awaken.

Outside my window the swollen tips of the branches attract my notice. Buds, waiting. Before very long their gray will redden, then burst in feathery yellow-green that will become long oval leaves for another season. Quite unconscious of me, the tree waits patiently to pursue its destiny. Merely by standing there, it touches one with the grateful sense of *place* in God's universe. So an ordinary wild ash tree, knobby and unbalanced, reveals just by its being there the power of God who gives forth all that is given. It focuses the universe that is gathered together by the designing wisdom of God. It flushes us with gratitude for the surprising goodness of God.

> The heavens declare the glory of God,
> the vault of heaven proclaims his handiwork;
> day discourses of it to day,
> night to night hands on the knowledge.
> No utterance at all, no speech,
> no sound that anyone can hear;
> yet their voice goes out through all the earth,
> and their message to the ends of the world.
> (Ps. 19:1–4, JB)

12. Time has passed. It is another morning now as I write, bright and sunny but still cold. The wisps of snow that highlighted the bends and branches of my ash tree have evaporated, and the tree itself has dried to mere gray. It stands there opaque, in all frankness merely itself. That moment of recognition is gone.

Time has passed. Something is lost. Has something been gained? Perhaps. But the time itself cannot be retrieved. With the passing of time I recognize in myself a vague, sad feeling—regret? I sense as well a slight tightness like fear. Do you know the feeling?

Time passes, and there is no turning back. We ride time like a raft riding a river, hardly in control, constantly flowing fast or sluggishly onward toward inevitable sea.

> All streams run to the sea,
> but the sea is not full;
> to the place where the streams flow,
> there they flow again.
> All things are full of weariness;
> a man cannot utter it.
> (Eccles. 1:7–8, RSV)

With time we are passing away. Yet there is a joy in the passing of time. Perhaps it is here that music finds its inspiration. Does it sing to us out of the flowing of time, hinting of the mystery of time? We ride this same river all together. Yes, we have passed this same way, say all of the writers and singers of history and those who have not been noticed by history. In the passing of time we find kinship with all of humankind.

Sadness and fear I understand, for in the passing of time we are passing away. But joy? From what does the river of time flow forth? And is the sea toward which it flows merely a sea of death and forgetfulness? The passing of time remains a fearful, sad puzzle . . . without faith. But—in the beginning, God! . . . In the end?

> . . . then comes the end,
> when he hands over the kingdom to his God and Father. . . .
> When everything is subjected to him,
> then the Son himself will [also] be subjected
> to the one who subjected everything to him,
> so that God may be all in all.
> (1 Cor. 15:24, 28)

The flow of time begins from God; it is the work of God; it is to end in God. Then the inevitable, gentle press that we feel each moment reveals that we are caught up in that current of creation and salvation. The current is not rushing blindly. It flows forth from the creative power of God. In its flowing, guided by the work of God's Word, it gathers the Kingdom. In its passing is a loving promise: we will not pass away! We will pass over together into immortal and imperishable being with God.

No wonder the passing of time inspires the most joyful of the arts!

13. I'm at my window again. A flash of vermilion draws my attention again to the ash tree. A cardinal comes to rest silently in the bowl formed by three twigs at the end of a branch. His mate flits to the branch above. They seem to study the bowl—for a nest? Such different purposes and needs the ash tree serves!

The tree is the focus of a complex economy. The melting snow, obedient to merely physical laws of gravity and temperature, passes into the earth to meet the tree's roots. There, when the time is right, the living roots will draw moisture and nourishment upward. Buds will unfurl into leaves which gather the power of the sun and which later fall to re-form the nourishing earth (at least those that my busy rake will miss). Meanwhile insects will take for granted that branches and trunk are their thoroughfares. Perhaps the cardinals will return to rest in the branches and to feast on the insects. And from time to time I in my window will watch with fascination, drawn by the tree to sense a larger world and to yearn toward a still higher reality, beyond the passing of time. And now I share with you that watching and that yearning.

Everything opens upward . . .

> For creation awaits with eager expectation
> the revelation of the children of God.
> (Rom. 8:19)

Like a spiritual seed, the yearning for God impregnates every level of being in the universe. As if in labor, elements combine ever more richly. Life emerges to reach by unfolding branch or unfurling wing ever higher toward awareness. Humankind arrives to gather the longing of creation into yearning, then recognition, then praise.

> Oh, the depth of the riches and wisdom and knowledge of God!
> How inscrutable are his judgments and how unsearchable his ways!
> (Rom. 11:33)

14. The whole world around us is caught up in this dynamic mystery of being and of time. Everything comes forth into being out of the power of God. Everything in the world stands, poised, reflecting the intricate and boundless creative wisdom of God. At the same time everything is bound together by strands of destiny which draw toward unity with God.

Why is there anything at all? Why among all possibilities for a universe has there emerged a place in which the likes of humankind might be drawn to wonder by the flash of a cardinal's wing on an ash bough?

And how tiny a place this is in the unfolding universe of galaxies upon galaxies, which are revealed through ever more sophisticated instruments to ever more highly trained investigators by something so simple, obvious yet incomprehensible as—light! Light like the flame of a small candle: constantly it emerges as from an upward-flowing fountain, yet stands apparently stable in its familiar swirled shape. Always and constantly, though, it reaches and flies upward. Everything, from tiniest particle to most distant galaxy, is constantly emerging, reflecting, returning.

> For from him and through him and for him are all things. To him
> be glory forever. (Rom. 11:36)

On this sharply colder day frost has formed on my window, partly obscuring the ash tree with icy lacework. Even in this dormant season, the world has beautiful surprises for us: numberless variations on the simplest things, and numberless kinds of things within easy vision—unimaginable variety within the unity of imaginable horizons. Why should moisture, condensing and freezing on a window, form swirling feathers and radiating stars? Why in everything natural does form flow over the bounds of what is needed for function, so that beauty glows even on a stark winter day? Everything overflows itself, drawing us inward and upward into God.

In that overflow of beauty, do the things around us address us, call us? There is more at work in beauty than a moment's reflective pleasure. The tree, the cold and the condensing moisture are caught up in the current of creation and salvation, in the flow of time that begins from God, are the work of God, tend into God: "All creation is groaning in labor pains even until now" (Rom. 8:22). Is that the power of beauty—that in beauty we are drawn dramatically through the things around us to recognize the power, presence and goodness of God? And in that joyful flash within *us*, do the tree and the frost find the completion of *their* destinies?

When we gather at the Lord's table and present ourselves as his people, then the natural world gathers with us. There our ordinary lives are caught up in union with Mary, the apostles, martyrs, and all the saints, in union with the other ordinary people around us and throughout the world, in union with everything that touches our lives and that we touch with our lives.

Everything opens upward!

15. We could make a big mistake at this point in our reflections. It is a pleasant thing to gaze out a window and savor beauty. We can enjoy sweet, restful feelings before we return to tasks at hand. We might (at least I must admit that *I* might) even gently wag our heads in pity on those who don't bother to indulge themselves in such interludes. What a foolish misunderstanding!

Such contemplation is not a pleasant luxury. It is an *obligation*! The natural world around us *demands* that we recognize it for what it is—coming forth from God, unique and irreplaceable, reflecting God in its beauty, reaching toward God by meeting our needs and by calling us to praise God through it. If we fail, imprisoned in our busyness, we do violence to the world by thwarting the work of God! We do violence to ourselves as well, making ourselves blind to beauty, deaf to harmony, dumb in the concert of praise, fools in missing the point of everything! (For everything opens upward . . .)

Of course, we won't *notice* how we have mutilated ourselves and thwarted our world—until the world itself begins to rise up against us. All around us, the world's uprising demands that we take notice. The earth returns to us the consequences of our thoughtless

exploitation. It returns to us the poisons we heedlessly discard. Its
soil grows weary and windblown. Its resources thin and wither.

> Yes, the hope of the godless is like chaff carried on the wind,
> like fine spray driven by the gale; . . .
> [The Most High] will forge a biting sword of his stern wrath,
> and the universe will march with him to fight the reckless.
> (Wisd. 5:14, 20; JB)

It is not enough to contemplate. We have to recognize the world
for what it is, and we must treat the things of earth accordingly—
with reverence, wonder and grateful stewardship.

> Lord, what variety you have created,
> arranging everything so wisely!
> Earth is completely full of the things you have made: . . .
> All creatures depend on you
> to feed them throughout the year; . . .
> You turn your face away, they suffer,
> you stop their breath, they die and revert to dust.
> You give breath, fresh life begins,
> you keep renewing the world.
> (Ps. 104:24, 27, 29–30; JB)

Body

This chapter will continue the journey into God
by recognizing God's presence hidden in what happens
within our body when we perceive the world around us.

1. So far in our journey, we have found the power, presence and goodness of God revealed in something as ordinary as an ash tree in winter. We have also found how important it is to respect the ordinary natural things around us, things we often take for granted and overlook.

Thought of the ash tree has sent me to my window again. As I gaze at that same tree now, I note that patches of matted gray-green grass appear between the rounded white ridges formed by drifting winds. The sky is bright blue, and mud edges the driveway—frozen hard now, it will be soft and squishy by this afternoon. Standing within the window, I sense with my skin the gentle warm stirring of sun-heated air. Inhaling, I notice a fresh moistness in the air. In my body I sense a vague longing for spring. There—that is another dimension of our being that we tend to take for granted and overlook: our body's ordinary awareness. At this second stage of our journey, we need first to revitalize our bodily awareness. For the body too is good, revealing God, and destined not just for decay but for resurrection. And our bodily being is good, emerging from earth and rising in frank earthiness toward oneness with God in the body of Christ. It is our bodily being that locates us in a particular place and time, perhaps just inside a window overlooking an ash tree and a little urban valley that is just beginning to thaw.

This step in our journey is a step closer to ourselves, a step deeper into the mystery of our being in God's world, and a step higher in the return to God. It is part of the reflective prayer by which we seek to gather the flow of our lives and savor what is really happening within and around us.

2. Try now to become conscious simply of being where you are. As I do so, I am seated now, still close to my window of course. The

pressure of my body against the chair, the gentle current of air on
my skin, the muffled swish of sound from the street, the faint odors
of books and food and people, all these constantly remind me that
I am here, in the world at this particular place in this particular
time. I am connected to the world. I have a place. I am at home
here.

How reassuring, and yet how limiting. Our bodies constantly,
gently, remind us that we are not everywhere, not timeless. If our
thoughts are airily abstract and seek to escape our place and time,
then they become unreal, foolish—proud?

So by my body I am put in my place! It is a small place within a
large universe, but it is a real place. When we take a moment to
allow it to, the body patiently reminds us of our connection to Here
and Now by sight, sound, smell, taste and touch, and by its (usually)
quiet inner workings. Yet we can know, even *sense*, that Here is
within a universe that reaches out beyond streets and rivers and
lands and seas and even stars. Here also embraces invisible
thoughts and powers beyond any physical measure which may
touch us in ways we cannot know (or that we have forgotten how
to know). And we can know, even sense, that Now rides an ongoing
current emerging from primal nothingness and reaching . . . beyond.

Our place is fearfully small. The universe of space and time is
terribly vast and, from all appearances, ominously empty beyond
our little planet. But I have heard, and I believe, that this wide
universe of many layers is the design of God, and that this history
of many ages forgotten and to come catches us up all together into
the plan of God. This little place of ours is here within the design
of God, caught up with all humankind in the plan of God.

The body gently reminds us—fear at the enveloping, cavernous
darkness of space and time, falling! And like the body's own jerking
reflex in a falling dream, grasping and reaching out, Ah! . . . Oh,
of course, as ever, there is God, all around and beneath and above
and behind and ahead.

> . . . indeed he is not far from any one of us.
> For 'In him we live and move and have our being.'
> (Acts 17:27, 28)

3. It may take some effort to allow the body to share its awareness
with us. We tend to be busy about things to do, future things, or to
be worried or embarrassed about past things. With our consciousness so thrown ahead of or behind us, the body's present awareness
tends not to register. So we have to stop, even for a moment, which

may be all the time we have. We must call in the forays of the mind . . . and rest.

How? Off it goes again, this busy mind of mine. The children are up! Oh, no, I forgot to mix the orange juice last night! The garbage has to go out—I think I hear the truck coming! Am I ready for class? Oh, gosh! I have an early appointment!

Just for a moment or three, TURN IT OFF!

Sit! Sit straight but not stiff, still but alert, like the way you have to sit while driving a long distance on a highway. Close your eyes. Take a deep breath, and then just let the air fall out, puff! And with it, let go of all the busyness—Puff! Try it!

Relax.

Then focus, concentrate, on just one sense. Try the sense most overlooked, touch. If you are sitting, allow yourself slowly to feel the pressure of your body against the chair . . . then the pressure of your hands against your lap, against each other ... of your feet against the floor . . . concentrate, now. Can you feel the gentle closeness of your clothing against your knees and thighs? . . . Can you feel the subtle changes of your clothing's pressure on chest and stomach as you breathe? . . . Can you now feel the silent touch of air upon the fine hairs of your neck and face? . . . Focus even more closely now, upon the soft, cool current of air entering your nostrils as you breathe. Concentrate. Turn off everything else. Keep trying, in what moments you can make or take, until you can *feel* again. Feel the quiet, constant rhythm of air in your nostrils . . .

In such a way our sense of touch can dramatically reveal the vital connection of our own being to the world, in so simple a thing as the gentle current of air that constantly flows in and out through our nostrils. And without that air? We are such fragile and precarious creatures! Again, with a choke, the body grasps, reaches out.

There is God.

So the sense of touch brings awareness of our self, of our location in the world, of our dependence and fragility—and almost by reflex this awareness opens upward, reaching toward God.

So we can awaken our body's awareness by taking a few minutes wherever we can find them, concentrating on each sense in turn. Our hearing, if we turn off our busyness and just let the present sounds of our world flow over us and immerse us, can reveal our links with the surrounding world and our smallness. Taste tells us closely of our body's meeting with another reality. And then, of course, we can open our eyes and perhaps really see. With all of our senses, our being opens outward to our world, and our being in the world opens upward into God.[1]

4. Through such reflection, little by little over time, we can reawaken our bodily awareness. If we do so, two very simple facts should gradually become obvious to us, facts so simple that they have befuddled philosophers ever since the time of Descartes.

The first simple fact is that there is no sharp chasm separating the earthy, material being of my body from rational thinking and spiritual upreaching. If our awareness is habitually limited to the rational, that is *not* because we are such eminently rational beings. Rather it is because we may have allowed ourselves (helped by the bias of our culture) to become forgetful of bodily awareness. For abstract philosophy, the human oneness of spirit and matter has been a virtually insoluble problem. For ordinary concrete awareness, it is an obvious given.

The second simple fact is that there is no unbridgeable gulf separating our own being and awareness from our world. The press of my body against the chair is no projection or illusion. The vital link of my being with the environment is absurdly obvious in that rhythmic current passing through my nostrils. The body's awareness affirms clearly that we are *in* the world, inseparably *with* the full range of its realities. But when philosophy forgets concrete bodily awareness and in airy abstraction seeks instead to escape place and time and person and community, fleeing into disembodied words, then thought becomes unreal, fruitless, foolish.

Bodily awareness testifies therefore to the integrity of our being, and to the unity of our being with the world. It is an essential step in this second stage of our journey into God.

5. You may experience a tingling pleasure as you bring your body's awareness into focus. Indeed, the felt sense of your actual being in the Here and Now may prompt a shudder of joy. I felt such pleasure gazing out my window when the red flash of the cardinal's wing focused and balanced a scene of grays and whites and pale blue. Again I felt such pleasure as the sun warmed the air about me, gently calling forth the spring outside while awakening my body's awareness within. A shudder of joy rose for me from the constant gentle current of air in my nostrils. Have you felt such quiet pleasures too? It is good that we are here.

The immense power of the universe approaches us proportioned to our body's awareness. Within the world even chance patterns snap suddenly to balance and beauty. And even in tiny ways the world is good to us, a home for us. Power . . . beauty . . . goodness . . .

What is man that you should be mindful of him,
    or the son of man that you should care for him?
You have made him little less than the angels,
    and crowned him with glory and honor.
You have given him rule over the works of your hands,
    putting all things under his feet. . . .
O LORD, our Lord,
    how glorious is your name over all the earth!
(Ps. 8:5–7, 10)

6. Once we have begun to reawaken our bodily awareness, next we need to become more conscious of the links which bind that awareness to the other dimensions of our inner being. This is yet another step closer to ourselves, deeper into the mystery of our being in God's world, and higher in the return to God.

The pleasure and joy that we feel are an important sign. Why pleasure, and why joy? Joy came with the flash of color that balanced a scene into a vision. It came with warmth that testified to the proper recurrence of spring. It came with the constant current of air which quietly ensures that in the universe we are at home. That joy was not a response to the harmony of a world *outside* of us. The harmony includes us. More than that—the harmony *happens* as we meet the world, and it rises out of that meeting.

For the gray ash tree knows nothing of the fading whiteness of the snow, of the blue of the sky, nor even of the cardinal's wings. The cardinal in turn flies only to catch a meal. They know nothing of each other, nor of the wholeness of the world which is their setting. They are simply and unconsciously there—until in my gaze they are recognized in their harmony and wholeness.

These things, these things were here and but the beholder
Wanting; which two when they once meet,
The heart rears wings bold and bolder
And hurls for him, O half hurls earth for him off under his feet.
(Gerard Manley Hopkins)[2]

In this meeting, we and the things of earth have a kind of partnership. The world's own harmony—its being as world, the unity of its universe—is recognized only in the meeting. The pleasure and joy come not just from our being able to sneak a peek at a harmony already there, apart from us. They arise in our perceptions when that harmony *happens*, the product of a successful partnership between ourselves and the world.

7. And look at the pattern of that partnership! As an example, let me use the experience I described to you earlier. In that experience, tree, snow, bird, hill and horizon sent themselves forth

to me and embraced me, with their mystery of world and universe all unspoken. I stood here in my window, merely receiving and accepting, until something like a bird's red flight happened to snap me to awareness. Then I turned. In a flash of recognition the world suddenly was intelligible as world, and the universe appeared in its unity. Out of that recognition came pleasure and joy . . . and praise.

> Sing to the LORD a new song;
>   sing to the LORD, all you lands.
> (Ps. 96:1)

What is happening? Mystery sends itself forth; it presents itself in mind and word; in joy the union of world is complete.

Do you feel another flash of recognition?

Trinity!

Why should we be surprised to find that the pattern of partnership that binds us to our world echoes the Trinity pattern of God's own being? Everything opens upward—to the Father, who as fountain-source sends himself forth into Word, and the timeless flash of love binding them in unity is the same Spirit which draws us ever closer, deeper, higher into God. Everything opens upward, now by its echo of the dynamism of divine life. That echo hints that, just as we are embraced in the harmony of the universe, so we are caught up and drawn home by the constant gentle current of grace. We are drawn to the Father, through Jesus the Word, by the power of the Spirit.

We are reminded of this embrace of Trinity every time we become aware of our being in the world. Well, at least we *can* be reminded—because it is *there.* Yes, it may seem awkward or artificial to look for it at first. But if you do seek it, you will notice it. Then gradually this embrace of Trinity will become constant within your awareness.

8. But there is more happening here than just an echo and a footprint. Let me return again to that experience I described for you. The cardinal's wing flashed only a moment, and in that moment there was for me a vision of harmony that spoke of the wholeness of the world. But then it was gone, and the rapt pleasure that I felt lasted but a moment longer. Then it became only a memory, tinged with the sadness of passing away.

Were I a skilled artist, I would want to capture that moment on a canvas. Indeed I would feel called, even driven to do so. And the canvas could catch the gray, the faded white and the blue balanced by the flash of red. I would want to show it to you and hope that you would see not just colors, and not even just the balance, but the vision of harmony and wholeness. Would you see it? All of it?

Perhaps. But even then, the joy would be bittersweet, tinged by the poignant realization that

> I have seen all things that are done under the sun,
> and behold, all is vanity and a chase after wind.
> (Eccles. 1:14)

Is there no joy that is not surrounded by sadness? Even if by some magic we could hold that entire moment still, we would not find full and restful joy in it. For it was not just the balance of shapes and colors that brought joy. It was that in this balance, for a moment, the harmony of world and the unity of universe *happened.* Where did I see *that?* Could someone ever catch *that* on canvas?

In the partnership of perception where we recognize world and universe, we do not perceive harmony and unity as objects, nor do we project them as merely subjective wish or hope. When we recognize harmony in the balance of colors, our recognition is reaching beyond just this time and this place. And when we realize that the horizon which limits our vision is not an end but rather opens beyond any end, even beyond the farthest star—then our realization is reaching into the infinite.

So the process of simple perception consciously, or (usually) unconsciously, reveals that our being Here and Now is not imprisoned by time and space. In every perception, our mind locates itself in relation to the timeless and the infinite. Hence the pleasure and the poignancy of each moment of beauty is a promise—that restful joy can come only beyond any tangible goal, beyond the finite:

> You are great, O Lord. . . .
> You have made us for yourself,
> And our heart is restless
> until it rests in you.
> (St. Augustine *Confessions* 1,1)[3]

Now we can see that there is more happening here than a mere echo or footprint of the pattern of God's own life. There is also, within that reflection, a reaching and a call.

Everything *draws us* upward . . .

9. My wife came into the room, wondering why, when I claim to be at work, I spend so much time staring out the window. (I expect you may have wondered that too.)

"Look," I said.

The cardinal was still there, perched within bowl-shaped twigs at a branch end. Suddenly he flew away in a flash of scarlet.

"Oh!" And her hand, joined to mine, tightened slightly. Did she understand? Have you understood, as you have read? Can one understand the moment of a vision of harmony, of wholeness of world, of unity of universe? Does anyone understand the vision behind the work of art? We do use the words. And you *do* know what the words mean, don't you? From the imperfect words you do understand—at least enough to realize a little what happened to me in that moment of recognition.

It is astonishing, though obvious, that we can speak of our most private, intimate bodily awareness and be understood. Indeed, isn't it the most intensely personal, private and unique elements of our lives—our growth and decline, our sexual awakening and love, our bodily fears of danger and death, our reaching beyond—that are the most universal? The whole library of the world's literature affirms that.

It is astonishing that we can communicate. Not just that we can hold commerce, but that we can share awareness and vision and joy—enough at least to build love on, to bring persons to their humanity in our families, to form peoples and cultures, to be one world!

For each person's awareness *is* unique! Each culture is different, and each era is different. The same words mean different things to different people and different times. Philosophers struggle for precise, unambiguous, disembodied words that are universally understood—and they fail.

Yet among all the differences and out of all the gaps of understanding and through all the failures in communication there emerges, right in our bodily awareness, a universal truth beyond words. That truth makes possible all our efforts and promises to redeem all our failures. That truth is simply *there* in our bodily awareness, *felt* in our concrete relation to our world. Some of our words reach toward it: "harmony," "wholeness of world," "unity of universe." Words reach to the timeless and the infinite. But words do not touch it.

In our bodily awareness *everything together draws us upward,* and that is the constant, universal, unspoken ground of all our awareness! The reach toward God is therefore not just an occasional prayer launched from our earthbound being. In *every* perception we are caught up into Trinity.

10. Is this why literature, art, music and dance are perennially a fountain of renewal for the human community? They make us notice the universality that, by habit or by resolve, we tend to repress. They reveal the common reach to God that binds the universe into unity. So it is the reach to God that sparks the pleasure we feel in response to beauty, the joy we feel in the world's

harmony, and the flash of recognition we feel when we become fully conscious of the universe around us.

But that flash of recognition is also at the root of any creative act or insight. From that basic reach to God springs the joy, excitement and resolve that a mathematician feels as the mind pursues the elegant proof; that the medical researcher feels as a pattern emerges which promises cure for a disease; that the engineer feels when a design works; that the writer feels when words blend and flow to capture thought; that a teacher feels when students actually begin to understand; that a manager feels when a strategy succeeds; that a parent feels when a child shows a spark of real character.

That fundamental reach to God is the constant in the variety of our perceptions. It is the real reason for the joy that flushes our body in response to a flash of scarlet amid the grays and blue of a late winter day. Everything opens upward! Even in our bodily awareness we are caught up in the quiet powerful current of the love of God.

11. We have traveled now through the second stage of our journey. We began with the world of things, and then we discovered what happens when the world and our awareness meet in partnership. Now we can appreciate how all the creatures of the world open upward toward God. Now we can sense how the world and we within it are caught up in the current that flows from God as fountain-source, that takes shape in body and object and word, that soars back to God in recognition and praise.

It has taken no special sophistication to recognize these things, nor lengthy education, nor extraordinary spiritual insight. Ordinary things ordinarily presented to ordinary people such as we are—that's all it has taken. Plus the willingness to open our awareness! Those ordinary things are so close to us that we most often miss them or take them for granted. Everything opens upward, always, constantly drawing us into God.

12. If that is the case, though, how are we to get the dishes washed and the car fixed and the grocery shopping done? Perhaps it is just as well that this awareness usually remains unconscious and breaks through only in momentary flashes of recognition. And yet it is there—a sense of that quiet, powerful current like our sense of the swirling and surrounding air.

Sometimes, though, things are presented to us in ways that should evoke special recognition. Some things open upward in special ways. The ordinary loaf of Italian bread my family had with dinner was particularly tasty. In the pleasure I felt in its taste, I sensed also the glow of our being family, our being together and at home in the world. A still-life painting of a loaf of bread is less ordinary. It makes us pause and regard the loaf for itself and not just as something to eat. Bread is so basic, so clearly the nourishing gift of earth. The painting calls us to contemplation, to the recognition of the power, wisdom and goodness of the universe focused in this image of bread.

A story in the Book of Exodus opens another level of recognition. The people of Israel, freshly escaped from Pharaoh, are now without food in the desert. They are not happy about it. "Then the LORD said to Moses, 'I will now rain down bread from heaven for you' " (Exod. 16:4). Bread is the gift of God, tangible evidence that he cares for his people.

And then something very ordinary and yet incredibly astonishing: "The Lord Jesus, on the night he was handed over, took bread, and, after he had given thanks, broke it and said, 'This is my body that is for you. Do this in remembrance of me' " (1 Cor. 11:23–24).

We gather, often quite forgetful, at the table of the Lord's Supper. We gather as Christ's body, the presence of Christ within our own bodies. We gather as God's people, family, together with Mary, the apostles and martyrs and all the saints. The earth itself is gathered too, in the bread which is the fruit of the earth and work of human hands. Here in the sacrament all levels of meaning are compressed and then explode outward and upward, resonating from the earthy inner working of our bodies all the way to the astonishing oneness of ourselves with Christ and of Christ with God.

13. So it is that

> ever since God created the world his everlasting power and deity— however invisible—have been there for the mind to see in the things he has made. (Rom. 1:20, JB)

These things were here, and but the beholder wanting. But is the beholder always able to see?

If we are forgetful, we can be reminded, awakened. Then, flushed with the joy of recognition, we may reach out to others, to remind and awaken them. Be prepared for a rebuff.

In these stages of our journey, what we have come to know solves no problems, makes no profits, shows no empirical evidence, produces no measurable results. Therefore, some people in our society will judge that our journey leads nowhere, that it is useless. Bonaventure echoes Paul's judgment of that attitude: "Such people are without excuse: they knew God and yet refused to honor him as God or to thank him; instead, they made nonsense out of logic and their empty minds were darkened" (Rom. 1:20–21, JB).

Then let's scream judgment against those who fail to echo our joy!

Wait. Have we forgotten our own forgetfulness? Have we forgotten that we had to make a serious commitment even to begin this journey? Have we forgotten what a struggle it has been to travel through just these early stages of our journey? We have had to be patient with ourselves. We must also be patient with others.

But those closed attitudes thwart the spiritual destiny of the earth. They lead directly to the kind of exploitation, neglect and pollution that threaten to thwart the very physical survival of the earth. To be patient does not mean to be passive. It means to avoid destructive anger and, rather, to act with single-minded persistence. These stages of our journey into God, therefore, move us also toward action to respect and sustain the earth. The journey into God is also a journey of active mission into our world.

Thought and Action

In this chapter our journey steps within,
discovering the image of God
through the workings of our personal being.

1. Our journey so far has been bright with the world's light, a light that glows within our bodies in the partnership of mind and world that we call perception. But now our journey turns inward, into the sanctuary of ourselves as persons. The eyes of our imagination have to adjust to a light like that in Gothic churches—the blue of stained glass, the quivering yellow of many candles, and, deep inside, the small red glow announcing the divine presence.

Pass through this door, then, into the inner sanctuary of the self. Perhaps it would be good to find a quiet place where we can sit comfortably and close our eyes. Earlier we sought in this way to become aware again of our bodily being. Now we need to reach inward and upward from that bodily awareness, so that we can reach toward whatever it is that we mean most deeply when we say "I."

Who, what, is "I"? Of all questions, that should be easy for us to answer! We are each the world's foremost expert on "I," aren't we? After all, who is closer to myself than "I"?

But it is not an easy question to answer, after all. On the one hand, plenty of answers rush forth: I am a man, son to my parents, husband to my wife, father to my children. I am a citizen of my nation, my state, and my city. I own various things and owe various debts. But answers such as these describe our *roles*, not the very self.

Who, what is "I," *really?* Something within me fights the question. Is it the wrong question? Is the "I" a reality that remains hidden from one who seeks it directly?

> For whoever wishes to save his life will lose it,
> but whoever loses his life for my sake will save it.
> (Luke 9:24)

Bonaventure says simply to look within, and you will see that your soul loves itself dearly because it knows itself, and it knows itself because it is deeply mindful of itself. Bonaventure found the image of God there, in that inner dynamism of memory, knowledge and love.

Can it be so direct and clear? I find my own emotions more mixed, my sense of self more ambiguous. Is that true for you as well?

2. Let me share with you several personal experiences that have led me upward through this stage of the journey. Perhaps similar patterns or events fill your own life. Then, as we reflect on such experiences with Bonaventure's help, perhaps we will see how they open upward as a path into God.

Several days ago I sat, tired, half listening to the radio. Suddenly I realized that I was hearing a piece of music that had been important to me when I was young and struggling to establish my identity. As I listened, a flood of memory arose beneath words, memory not of particular events so much as of being with others and hoping and doing. With that memory I recognized a continuity: the wanderings of my life have indeed been a path to the present, and they open to a particular future. Then a feeling welled up in me: it is good to be here, to be me. But the feeling was tinged with a sense of emptiness and disappointment as well. In spite of so much ambiguity, after all, perhaps it is good—I hope.

Bonaventure points out the echo of Trinity in such an experience of self: From memory as fountain-source there emerges a wordless sense. Intellectual recognition traces it and names it into Word. Then emotion and will connect it and claim it in Love.

But the taste seems bittersweet. Is *this* supposed to be the image of God in us? Yes, Bonaventure would say, remembering insights of his own teacher, St. Augustine. For what really makes the inner self an image of God is that in memory, knowledge and love of self, a person is drawn to reach beyond the self toward God. The mark of the image of God in us is that our hearts are restless until they rest in God.[1] Is that why our sense of self is poignant, unsatisfied? We might think it is so because we are so *far* from being an image of God. But is it because the place of rest is not here in the self? This is but an image, drawing beyond.

3. That kind of experience is rather rare, I must admit. Much more frequently I sense who I am in this way: work has to be done, and "I" am the one who has to do it! Such is the lay life. Does that mean our paths separate here from the solitary meditation favored by Brother Bonaventure?

Not necessarily. Let's look more closely at a typical weekend task. On this weekend, I have to spade my garden and get it ready for spring planting. Otherwise, my family will miss the fresh tomatoes, peppers and broccoli that keep us eating well through the late summer and fall. What a mess my garden is! Brown stalks and tangles from last year mix with the impudent bright green of new weeds and the dirty gray of newspapers that winter has blown into the tangle. I survey the garden plot, estimate what needs to be accomplished and what tools I'll need, take a deep breath, and set myself to do it.

When the sun is low, my back aches and my hands are red. But that plot of ground has become a smooth, black space for planting. I sit on the porch steps, sip a cold beer and gaze at the garden, enjoying a sense of accomplishment because what I only imagined this morning is now a reality.

I began this morning with an intention: an intention rooted in my awareness of who I am, what my family's needs are and what my possibilities are. Then I put that intention into action, and struggled with the resisting earth to make real what had only been internal to me. Now I gaze upon the unity of intention and reality, and I am mellow with satisfaction. It is good for us to be here. Out of the mystery of the Father's divine intention the Word came forth to struggle with the resistant world, so that by the power of the Spirit all things may be brought together within the reign of God, in heaven and on earth.

Does this mean that even here, in something as simple as spading a garden, we are acting out the image of God? Yes. Everything opens upward, everything!

But such mellow recognition of the image of God does not last long. Other tasks demand our attention. And those weeds will return . . . This is not the place of rest. This is only a glimpse, drawing beyond. If we try to hang on to such a moment, we spoil it. After all, the image of God is there in the *doing.* Perhaps at one moment or another, surprised, we will glimpse it consciously.

4. Some tasks are too big for one person. Such tasks open up another dimension of this stage of our journey.

I stood one afternoon worrying over a tall, crooked locust tree crowding the narrow space between my family's house and the house next door. It had to go. My neighbors, Pat and Felipe, happened by.

"Big job," I muttered. "I'm afraid of it, so close to the house in one direction and the utility lines in the other."

We opened beers, looked at the tree and at each other.

"We can lower that phone line," Felipe suggested. "Then it can fall clear."

Sure! That would work. My worry was transformed to grateful resolve. Out came saw, rope and ladder.

Pat climbed the ladder to loosen the phone line and to set the rope (I get vertigo even on a stepladder). We played out the rope in the direction we wanted the tree to fall, Pat grabbed the saw, Felipe and I stationed ourselves on the safe end of the rope, and we set to work. The tree began to give—but the wrong way! The chain saw jammed. "Pull hard!" Pat yelled, and we heaved on the rope while the saw freed and cut further. The tree righted, swayed. Crack! Very slowly, then faster, the top moved in an arc that followed the rope line. Instinctively I found myself well back from the fall. With a clattering Whumpph! the tree hit the ground. We blinked and looked around. No damage to either house or to other trees. No utility lines snagged. Whew!

Yahoo! We did it! When we stopped shaking, we stood back, sipped our beers, and savored the special joy of a job shared and a job done.

Who, what is "I," *really?* I am husband to my wife, father to my children, neighbor and friend to my neighbors and friends. These are not mere roles; they are *relationships.* Who am "I" by myself? Just then, I really didn't care! I was too happy that *we* were being *we* together! What does it mean to be *we?* Sharing and enjoying a good piece of work brings us together effectively. What really happens as people share a task?

My neighbors and I began with a shared intention, an intention rooted in our awareness of what needed to be done and what we together were capable of doing. Then together we put that intention into action and struggled with a tree (which had other ideas) in order to realize our intention. Then we gazed together upon the results of our work, and we shared satisfaction.

Intention, action and resolution. Once again Trinity. But something more happens in such a shared task than happened when I spaded my garden alone. Now, not only is there joy in the realization of intention, but the bonds of neighbor to neighbor are strengthened, the bonds of friend to friend. Our work together not only reflects the dynamism of Trinity; it realizes, in a little way, the love community of Trinity.

Everything opens upward—and outward! At its deepest and its best, everything leads upward toward transcendence; everything leads outward toward community. But everything is at its deepest and best only seldom and then not for long. Often after the glow comes the fact of separation, a twinge of regret.

This is not the place of rest; it too calls beyond. Let it go, and let's be on our various ways along the journey. Some things are best left unsaid. But always and everywhere know that it is there, unspoken. Perhaps at one moment or another, surprised, we will glimpse it.

5. But that tree was the task only of an afternoon. Some doings take longer. Another dimension opens on this stage of our journey.

Quite some years ago a special sort of recognition passed between me and a certain young woman. Then strands of our lives began to touch and intertwine. Together we formed an intention that combined calling and commitment and vowed that our separate ways should join into one shared path along our journey. We knew each other—ourselves!—only partly and still do. We knew the way ahead not at all. But we set out. That intention of ours cleared a path with space for now three others to join, and all our ways are braided together for the time.

We began with hopes and expectations and plans. Then we struggled with the resistance of earth and of time and (especially) of ourselves. What we actually do and have done comes out somewhere other than our hopes and plans—often less, but sometimes surprisingly more. Usually what we actually do is a matter of spading a garden on this day, removing a tree on that. Only seldom do we step back and survey the whole path we travel together, and those may be times of disappointment and doubt or of recognition and joy.

Those are usually moments without much talking, but perhaps they are times of making love. Making love frankly realizes what is most important, and so bridges the doubts and makes disappointment trivial. Making love captures and celebrates the joy. Making love gathers and compresses all that we are together so that it explodes inward and upward and outward, a sacrament.

Meanwhile hopes and expectations and plans diminish in their seriousness. Unlike short, manageable projects like spading a garden, marriage and the raising of children do not arrive shortly at a clear and satisfying completion. We learn to expect less, the less to be disappointed and the more to be surprised:

> Better is one handful with tranquility
> than two with toil and a chase after wind!
> . . . Two are better than one. . . . If the one falls, the
> other will lift up his companion. Woe to the solitary
> man! For if he should fall, he has no one to lift him up.
> So also, if two sleep together, they keep each other
> warm. How can one alone keep warm?
> (Eccles. 4:6, 9–11)

With lower expectations, more space opens in us for the surprise and the gift.

Such long-term doings form the core of our lives. They reflect not only the dynamism of Trinity, as does spading a garden; they reflect not only the love community of Trinity, as does a shared task of friends. Such doings also overleap themselves, transcending what we as human beings are capable of intending, working at or achieving. They launch us by sheer faith into cooperating in God's creating, redeeming, reuniting. More deeply and more closely than ever, and virtually in spite of ourselves, we are caught up surprised in the life and love of God.

When, therefore, we follow our journey into the workings of our personal being, we discover again the image of God. Our sense of self—memory, recognition, emotion—reflects Trinity and draws us to reach toward God. Our work—intention, action, resolution— echoes the dynamism of God's acts for his people and yet leaves us restless, yearning. Working together adds fellowship that imitates the inner life of God, yet it passes and points beyond itself. Lifelong commitment launches us well beyond what we can know or plan or control, acting day by day in hope, bound together by love, rooted in faith.

6. There is more. I am also a teacher, a learner. Each of us is, in one way or another. I happen to be a college faculty member. Talk about work without clear results! Rooted in years of study and weeks and days of planning, I meet for a few weeks with a few people to travel together along a little course. In some, I recognize the light of insight. Papers fly and eyes grow bloodshot. The obscenity of grades. Then our travel together is over. Good-bye. See you again sometime, maybe.

Did they ever really find the path? Was the light real or only a momentary flicker? I will not know. I will not see the results of my action, the resolution of my intention. Here again one must act in hope.

As we act as teacher or as learner, what we do is larger and longer still than the doings on which we have been reflecting. I am student to my mentors, teacher to my students, in a long, living chain of learning that emerges from the beginning of human cultures and that reaches forward to the consummation of the Kingdom. I am part of a faculty, each of us with different training but with similar intention. Among us we reach out to every facet of our society and our world. Among us, we as teachers draw our students, and we as learners struggle to be drawn in our various ways into the journey of all humankind.

At its best, such a community of learners is also an image of God. Among us, in our various fields of study, we emerge from the gathered memory of the whole human community. Speaking and sharing our knowledge and insight, we make that heritage live in our society. From that recognition, awareness opens upward, returning in wonder.

Trinity again. Should that be surprising, if, as we discovered earlier, every mere perception reflects the pattern of Trinity? How much more then will entire fields of knowledge and communities of learning echo that pattern?

In a learning community at its best, all fields emerge as heritage, express themselves as teaching and learning, and finally reach outward and upward beyond themselves, building community and returning into God. But not all learning communities ever reach their best, and those that do reach it are few, and do not maintain it for long. More typically, each academic discipline seals itself away from others and jealously defends a narrow specialization. Students then, instead of growing as whole persons along their journey, find themselves cut into little compartments—and heaven help them if they mention a term from one discipline in a test for another! Bonaventure bitterly fought against the same kind of compartmentalization at the University of Paris in his day. It made him so angry that he called it Antichrist and Lucifer.[2]

If anyone thinks that in academic communities one finds a place of rest, an "ivory tower," obviously she or he is not familiar with academic communities. Here too is the struggle and the call beyond.

7. At this third stage of our journey, we are reflecting on the ordinary workings of our *personal* being in order to discover there the image of God. In our sense of self, in our solitary work, in teamwork, in the long-term commitment of marriage, and in the tradition of our learning, we can recognize three constant patterns.

First is the reliable certainty of our being in relation to others and to the world. Avoiding the dead-end quest for certainty in solitary consciousness, we discover ourselves best and most solidly in communion with others—particularly in work, in learning and in love. In our ordinary work, struggling against the resistance of things and sometimes of other people, we know without doubt that the world is real, independent of our attention and intention.

Second is the reliable connectedness of mind and world and of person with person. Estimates of what is needed to do a job, estimates even of which way a tree must fall, tend to work out, or, if they don't, to be marked by recognizable error. That is true of spading a garden or of calculating mathematically the place of invisible stars. Mind and world are in partnership. Moreover, mind and mind can join in partnership, communicating intention and so making teamwork possible, making friendship possible, and indeed love. This partnership is the reliable rational structure of our being in the world with others.

Third, in every step in this stage of the journey we find satisfaction only for a moment, and then restless longing: this is not the place of rest. Everything lights up, opens outward and upward, calling us beyond ourselves to communion and to transcendence. The journey leads onward—into God.

In our ordinary personal being, our work, our relationships, our commitments—here is our pathway. In our ordinary being in the world with others—here is an image of God in being, structure and longing; here everything lights and opens up for us the way into God.

That is, everything *can* become light and open. We are all *called* to communion and transcendence. As often as not we miss it. There is no inoculation or indoctrination that prevents us from being fools, at least some of the time. Then we are blind to the light, we become trapped and entangled, we lose our way.

> The shrewd man's wisdom gives him knowledge of his way,
>   but the folly of fools is their deception.
> (Prov. 14:8)

> Teach me, O Lord, your way
>   that I may walk in your truth;
>   direct my heart that it may fear your name.
> I will give thanks to you, O Lord my God,
>   with all my heart,
>   and I will glorify your name forever.
> (Ps. 86: 11–12)

4

Grace

In this chapter
our journey probes more deeply within our personal being,
discovering the image of God
through the workings of God within us.

1. As we closed the previous stage of our journey, we heard
Bonaventure's gentle warning to be careful lest we lose our way.

The weather outside my window today has reinforced the warning. Warm spring blooms yielded to noonday darkness. Branches
bent; clouds overhead rushed and swirled. A rumbling crack and
blue blinding flash sent me scrambling back; the house shook as
the wind whipped trees violently and rain lashed the window. Deep
down an instinct made me want to hide somewhere warm, dry and
quiet! When the rumblings and flashes grew distant, I could dare
to continue our journey, still a little shaky.

Where were we? We were looking at ourselves, weren't we? Such
bright blooms of "I" we found, glowing and reassuring like sunlit
daffodils. But sobering realizations come with a cold blue flash like
lightning. Our sense of self—memory, recognition, emotion—fills
us with anguish as often as not, and sometimes makes us want to
crawl away and hide. Our work? Intention, procrastination, disintegration leave us frustrated as often as fulfilled. Working together?
Add misunderstanding and conflict and alienation. Lifelong commitment? Talk about out of control! Teaching and learning? I
know full well the long-term results of my efforts in most cases—
zilch, both in the blank faces of students wishing they were somewhere else and in my own confused and fading insight. Isn't
everything supposed to open upward? But a good hard look at
ourselves reveals that the bottom can drop out of everything too.
Instead of rising into God, we find ourselves slipping down splat! into
the muck that we thought was a garden before this rain: the muck of
the "I."

Have we been deluding ourselves? Have we really gotten anywhere at all on this journey into God?

I applied my mind to search and investigate in wisdom all things
that are done under the sun.
A thankless task God has appointed
for men to be busied about.
I have seen all things that are done under the sun, and behold, all is
vanity and a chase after wind. (Eccles. 1:13–14)

The journey has been pretty theoretical so far, hasn't it? This
academic way we have been taking is nice, because we can think all
kinds of pretty theoretical thoughts without ever really having to
face *our selves*! What delusion!

So I said to myself, if the fool's lot is to befall me also, why then
should I be wise? Where is the profit for me? And I concluded in my
heart that this too is vanity. . . . All is vanity and a chase after wind.
(Eccles. 2:15, 17)

We are hopelessly stuck in the muck of the "I." Oh, we can do our
meditations and ruminations, our readings and reflectings. We can
talk a good line to convince ourselves that we are good, upright,
even holy. But with one honest, lightning-flash look at ourselves, it
all comes tumbling down, splat! Oh, is there no way for us, after all?

What a wretched man I am! Who will rescue me from this body
doomed to death? (Rom. 7:24, JB)

2. When one has fallen down, he must lie there unless someone
lends a helping hand for him to rise.
Is that you, Brother Bonaventure? You've been dead seven
hundred and fifteen years. What makes you think you can help us
now?
It's not *I* who can help you . . .
Then go away! Leave us alone! Here we thought we could make
this journey. But we're stuck in the muck of our selves! It's hopeless!
We can't even move!
Of course you can't. But that's all right.
What?
That's all right. Neither could I.
You're a saint!
Laughter.
We are all riddled with self-deception!
So what? Look again.
At our *selves*? That's our *problem*!
You're not looking close enough.
What is closer to us than our selves?
God.

God? Oh, reflections and yearnings, maybe. Is that what you mean? But God is up there, out there, beyond. We can't reach . . . Look again.

We've *been* looking, and we see ourselves *thinking* that we reach up toward God, but actually we're fooling ourselves . . . Wait a minute.

> In this way the love of God was revealed to us: God sent his only Son into the world so that we might have life through him. In this is love: not that we have loved God, but that he loved us and sent his Son as expiation for our sins. (1 John 4:9–10)

Brother Bonaventure, do you mean that we've gotten it backwards? We thought we were here, reaching upward and outward, and God was there, beyond . . . But *Christ*: Christ shows that God is *within* us and among us!

More. Christ shows that you are caught up within God's love!

> But God proves his love for us in that while we were still sinners Christ died for us. (Rom. 5:8)

That is why Paul could turn so quickly from dismay in "this body doomed to death."

> Thanks be to God through Jesus Christ our Lord!
> (Rom. 7:25, JB)

Can *we* do that too? Can we so quickly come unstuck from this muck of the "I"?

Look around you.

We are here on the fourth stage of our journey. We are really here! Then . . . we *weren't* deceiving ourselves after all?

So what if you were? At the same time something else was happening. You did not climb by yourselves.

> In the same way, the Spirit too comes to the aid of our weakness; for we do not know how to pray as we ought, but the Spirit itself intercedes with inexpressible groanings. (Rom. 8:26)

All this way along the journey—searching the world around for signs of God, awakening our bodily awareness, and realizing what happens within when we perceive the world; our sense of self in our work with others, our commitments—all this way . . .

It was not your doing alone. The Spirit acts within you, empowering, illuminating, drawing.

We knew this before, didn't we? We knew that we are caught up in the power and goodness and love of God. What is different now?

You thought God was up there, and that you alone were doing

the climbing. Now you know how ridiculously you do on your own, compared with what God does within you.

But . . . how do we escape getting stuck in the muck of the "I" again and again?

Who says you escape that? Let go of reliance on yourselves; give yourselves by faith into Jesus. Let go of concern for your destiny; place your future by hope into Jesus. Let go of your need for security in yourselves; enter by love into Jesus. Then get on with your journey.

Easier said than done!

You forget who is doing it. Rise, and do not be afraid.

> I am the gate.
> Whoever enters through me will be saved,
> and will come in and go out
> and find pasture.
> (John 10:9)

3. After a storm the world glows in a strange gold light under the departing clouds. Battered daffodils stand straight and shine out like stars in the fertile dark green.

Such a turn our journey takes! Brother Bonaventure, where are we heading now?

Toward transformation.

Everything is different now, isn't it? Yet it has always been so, hasn't it? Only we fail to see it. We tend to think we are here, God is there—God *far* beyond us, we somewhere outside God! But Christ reveals that God is within and among us; we are within God. Everything that we are and that we do is at once our doing and the working of God in us. All our intentions and projects, riddled with self-deception, are taken up and transformed like poor bread into an acceptable offering. That's what you meant, Brother Bonaventure. It is all right, that muck of the "I"! We are safe and secure!

Are you now!

Oops, we did it again. Protecting the "I"! Is there any escape? This is ridiculous!

Yes, it is exactly that.

Then how are we to be sure that . . .

You need to be sure?

Honestly, we can't be sure whether we can be sure or not! But does that matter? We don't really *need* to be sure, do we? What do we need to do?

Seek God; seek the Kingdom. Set your face to go to Jerusalem.

The journey ahead is long still, rocky and uphill (see Luke 9:51–61; Mark 10:32).

We are to go onward in our journey. Onward—but Jerusalem . . . Golgotha! The place of the skull, the place of death! This journey is filled with *risk!* How can we go on without being sure?

Be watchful! Be alert! You do not know when the time will come (Mark 13:33).

But there *is* security after all! There's the heaven of reward, full of singing angels and pink and violet clouds. There's the heavenly Jerusalem, with walls of gold like glass. Everything is *safe* in heaven after all, isn't it?

Is it?

What! Even that is uncertain?

Do you need to be certain?

YES! Without a certain hope in heaven, then ahead there is . . . only darkness! How can we possibly go on without some kind of assurance?

Stop a moment: What are you looking at? Where is your concern? Aren't you still trying to protect that silly "I"? Look rather at what the Gospel says:

> Therefore I tell you, do not worry about your life, what you will eat [or drink], or about your body, what you will wear. . . . Your heavenly Father knows that you need them all. But seek first the kingdom [of God] and his righteousness, and all these things will be given you besides. (Matt. 6:25, 32–33)

Seek the Kingdom? Seek God's reign! Our own individual destiny is almost irrelevant, then. We are caught up in the Kingdom, the working of God bringing all things together in Christ. After all, the Scripture always calls us away from concern for self, toward sharing in what God is doing in Christ and in his body the Church.

Nothing matters then but Christ! Nothing matters but Christ!

For us to live then is to feel a powerful embrace, caught up in the current of the grace of God playing out the plan of God. We are gathered up in a great multitude which no man could number, from every nation, from all tribes and peoples and tongues (Rev. 7:9). We stand *as Church* before the throne, whirling together in a universal dance propelled by "the love that moves the sun and the other stars."[1]

What an astonishing gift!

4. New and surprising possibilities open up now, well beyond what we alone can do. Who cares about our weaknesses and ambiguities and confusions?

When we look at ourselves now, we can let go of the fearful need to protect and to be safe. Instead . . . look at us splattered in the sticky muck of the "I," spouting platitudes! How hilarious! What an incredible sense of humor God has! Weaknesses and ambiguities and confusions are themselves purified into prayer by the laughing embrace of God. "Thanks be to God through Jesus Christ our Lord!" (Rom. 7:25, JB).

And now we can understand that we do not understand, but we understand. We know that we do not know, but we know. The simple catechism certainties of childhood (and how intolerant a childhood many Catholics had!) have dissolved long ago. Perhaps in their place came a vague guilt and anxiety, as if by growing up we had somehow lost faith. But now we can let ourselves know that the doubts and the questions were also the work of God, calling and guiding to a light well beyond simple certainty.

When we look at others now, we should no longer feel that compulsion to search out their faults in order to protect ourselves. We no longer need to sniff for hypocrisy in order to justify our own ambiguity. If God accepts us in our ridiculousness, how should we fail to offer a laughing embrace to others?

> Beloved,
> if God so loved us,
> we also must love one another.
> (1 John 4:11)

The embrace of God's grace in Christ has smothered the folly of the self-grounded "I" marching doggedly toward a distant God. It makes irrelevant the inconsistencies we experience in the churches. It is God who acts always, acts close, acts within us and through us in spite of ourselves.

> What then shall we say to this? If God is for us, who can be against us? . . . I am convinced that neither death, nor life, nor angels, nor principalities, nor present things, nor future things, nor powers, nor height, nor depth, nor any other creature will be able to separate us from the love of God in Christ Jesus our Lord. (Rom. 8:31, 38–39)

We saw before that God has empowered us in our being, in our action, and in our sharing as his people. Now the power of God has ordered our inner spirit too. Everything within us opens upward; *everything*, even when the bottom seems to be falling out. Everything opens outward; *everything*, even when we feel shame and humiliation. The mystery of God is at work *in us*!

The power of God's love then is freeing. Are my intentions hindered by ambiguity, my work by obstacles? So what? Misunderstanding and conflict are no longer a threat to me, leading to alienation. Rather they lead to laughter and reconciliation. For nothing matters but Christ, and God is working in Christ even through our failures! Nothing can separate us from the love of God in Christ Jesus our Lord.

5. In the gold glow of grace, the Scriptures appear in a new light. We have heard the Scriptures in bits and pieces read of a Sunday, from a book that pastors and teachers said we should revere and obey—passages taken to prove a point, to impose a rule, or merely to decorate. But now the Scripture is so different!

The Bible tells of God's work in us and for us. He created the world so that it is very good. He chose a people (very ordinary people!) and guided them through nearly two millennia in spite of failures and infidelities. He embraced our history anew in Jesus, even to the depths of our weakness. He restores and empowers us almost in spite of ourselves. And he is bringing us together in and toward the full reign of God. This great story that spans all time and reaches to the edge of the universe is now *ours*, for the same God works the same way in us. Mary recognized that:

> The Mighty One has done great things for *me*, and holy is his name.
> (Luke 1:49, emphasis added)

For us, who are one in Christ's body the Church, Scripture is astonishing, humbling, empowering. How astonishing that Jesus, who is God beyond all bounds and uncreated Word beyond all comprehension, is closer to us than we are to ourselves. How humbling that Jesus, who is Lord and Judge of the universal Kingdom, like a brother and friend accepts us in all good humor with our failures and ambiguities. How empowering that Jesus, the firstborn of all creation, in whom all things were made and in whom the whole ordered plan of God is centered, bothers to transform our laughable ambiguities into the work of his love. But this is the Word of the Lord. (Thanks be to God!)

6. How then are we to hear and read the Scripture? First, we must let the Scripture speak on its own terms to us, let it puzzle and challenge us. Avoid the temptation to read meanings into Scripture according to our own preconceptions and wants. To avoid that, we'll need a little study and a little imagination, for we need to hear what the words were meant to say to those who first heard them. For instance, when Jesus speaks of the Good Samaritan (Luke 10:29–37), we need to hear with the ears of people who at that time *hated* Samaritans and thought that *nothing* good could *ever* come from a Samaritan. Then the parable is not just telling them to help

their neighbor; it is challenging them to recognize and abandon all their hatreds and prejudices. So we allow Scripture to speak to us on its own terms by learning about that original context of a passage of Scripture, and then by imaginatively placing ourselves in that context in order to hear the Word freshly as it was first meant.

With that original (literal) understanding of Scripture as a base, we can then allow the words of Scripture to take us up and guide us on our journey by their spiritual senses. For instance, in the story of the Good Samaritan a moral challenge confronts us. All of our prejudices and our preconceptions are subjected to judgment, and we are called to accept and love other persons without fears and reservations. This is a moral sense of Scripture, challenging us to reform and purify our lives.

The story also sheds light on the present meaning of Church as the Kingdom of God. By proclaiming the gospel, the Church is supposed to confront and confound the divisions of class and race and sex and ideology that form the fabric of society's prejudice. The Church is supposed to be unnerving, disturbing, prophetic— hardly comforting to the complacent. Here the Scripture speaks allegorically, connecting its story with the nature and vocation of Church. This sense of Scripture enlightens, giving us insight into the mystery we live as Church.

And the story looks forward to the fulfillment of the Kingdom, the fruition of God's ordered plan. Then the hated Samaritan will be revealed as good. Frustrations wrought by prejudice and hatred will be overcome, and the hidden transforming power of God at work in all our misunderstandings and ambiguities and failures will be manifest and evident to all (much to our own grateful surprise). In this mystical or anagogical sense, the Scripture lets us anticipate within ourselves the perfect joy of that fulfillment.

So the Scripture leads us on along our journey within our personal being where God is at work in us. It leads us by deep faith, firm hope and steadfast love to rest joyfully within a confidence in God that does not worry about the self. But our rest is that of one who sleeps aboard a moving ship, knowing where we have come from but barely imagining toward what this vibrant power is carrying us. For this stage of our journey is by no means the end. We are merely being prepared to enter realms beyond our imagination.

7. So we come to complete the part of our journey that has taken us within our personal being. We discovered the image of God in our sense of self: memory, recognition, emotion reflecting Trinity and drawing us to reach toward God. We discovered the image of

God in our work: intention, action, resolution echoing the dynamism of God's acts for his people and yet leaving us restless. We found it in working together, imitating the inner community of God's life. We found it in lifelong commitment, launching us beyond ourselves. We found our pathway to God here in our ordinary personal being as we work and love and learn with others. At its deepest and its best, everything in our personal being opens upward into transcendence. Everything opens outward into community.

But we tripped over the "I" trying to walk that path. Near despair, we discovered the simple and obvious fact that has been true all along: it is God who acts within us and for us, transforming our comical efforts by his power and wisdom and goodness. Embraced, we are caught up in God's ordered plan by faith and hope and love. We are guided by Scripture that is now lighted up for us. We are freed, and we are gathered into Church where God works for good in and through and in spite of our ridiculous limitations.

8. Look what has been done for us! Look what is happening within and among us! How completely astonishing!

> Hope does not disappoint, because the love of God has been
> poured out into our hearts through the holy Spirit that has been
> given to us. (Rom. 5:5)

We can go forward on our journey with real confidence now. Not that all ambiguities are removed, all failures prevented beforehand. There is no guarantee for us that we won't land flat like fools in the muck of the "I" again, and more than once! There is no guarantee that all will be harmony and inspiration in the churches. God likes a good laugh too much for that.

> But we hold this treasure in earthen vessels, that the surpassing
> power may be of God and not from us. (2 Cor. 4:7)

We can stand firm in our fellowship, then, in spite of ourselves and our weaknesses. Maybe *because* of them!

> I will rather boast most gladly of my weaknesses, in order that the
> power of Christ may dwell with me. Therefore, I am content with
> weaknesses, insults, hardships, persecutions, and constraints, for
> the sake of Christ; for when I am weak, then I am strong. (2 Cor.
> 12:9–10)

No need to feel insecure any more. No need to be defensive. No reason to cling to demands on ourselves, or to our expectations of others. Let go, just let go. Now we can feel free.

This is my commandment: love one another as I love you. No one has greater love than this, to lay down one's life for one's friends. (John 15:12–13)

Did we ever guess, as we heard that fearful challenge, that we might meet it well with laughter?

But in all this we are being led, being prepared for further steps in our journey. It is for a reason that we are strengthened through the Spirit, that we are given to recognize Christ dwelling in our hearts:

... that you, rooted and grounded in love, may have strength to comprehend with all the holy ones what is the breadth and length and height and depth, and to know the love of Christ that surpasses knowledge, so that you may be filled with all the fullness of God. (Eph. 3:17–19)

God beckons. Rise, and do not be afraid.

5

The One God

*In this chapter we seek to rise beyond ourselves
to contemplate the transcendent unity of God as Being.*

1. One peculiar thing about this spiritual journey is that we don't really seem to be *going* anywhere. The places we have already been stay with us. We continue to do the same kind of things in the same places we have been all along. Or are they the same, after all?

It is late spring now as I write, and here I am facing the tasks of another weekend. The lawn needs mowing. As I set about that task, I breathe air that is comfortably warm, laden with the purple scent of late lilacs and the heavy, sweet ivory of blooming arcs that hang from the honey locust trees above my head. So my bodily awareness enjoys this sense of place while my conscious mind aims the growling mower along its path. Fortunately mowing takes little conscious effort, so my mind is free to journey.

We have come a long way on our journey, haven't we? At this point Bonaventure compares the way we are traveling to a worshipper passing dreamlike through the ancient Temple of Jerusalem. There in the outer courtyard one could join in festive songs and prayers, in clear daylight surrounded by the visible world and alert to bodily awareness. Next we were invited into the sanctuary near the altar of sacrifice. By the glow of inner lamps we explored our personal being and found ourselves broken, but remade by Christ.

Now the high priest himself beckons us to follow up steep, wide stone steps to the forbidding veil of the Holy of Holies, where the majesty of God dwells. Trembling we pass through the veil into darkness. We sense rather than see the sacred Ark before us. Hovering on each side are the mythic Cherubim whose wings frame the overflowing emptiness of the Mercy Seat above the Ark, where the mystery of God dwells. From these Cherubim we hear the voices of those who have gone before us on the journey into God. By listening first to one and then to the other, we can hope to guide our eyes to vision in the darkness.

We have sought God in the presence of the earth. We have sought God in our presence to ourselves. Now are we to find God in the absence of everything?

Who and what is God, anyway? Images and ideas flit about our minds—pictures of a bearded old man in the sky, ideas of omnipotence and infinity. But these are in our mind, perhaps figments of our fantasy and delusions of wish-fulfillment. Who and what is God *really*? We call out into the darkness of the Holy of Holies.

Beyond the echoes of ourselves the response is only silence and emptiness. Darkness. Very deep within us lies a quiet terror. We have sought God, and now there is only . . . Darkness!

2. Many voices crowd our minds with talk about God. Much of what we hear is delusion, and we have to recognize and turn beyond those who have taken blind alleys rather than following the steep stony path of the journey into the darkness of God.

Some speak with bright familiarity of God. "The Lord told me," they say, or "God showed me," without the slightest trace of distance or doubt. Filled with confidence that they know Jesus as savior and friend, they fail to realize that he is at the same time Judge and God beyond limits. Missing the divine paradox, they stand way out in the bright outer court while thinking that they sit comfortably right in the Mercy Seat itself. What presumption! Those who really know God, like Isaiah or Jeremiah, call upon God's name with wonder—reluctantly, hesitantly. They know the silence and darkness of God.

Some others recognize the paradox of all talk about God and conclude, limited by a narrow logic, that such talk therefore makes no sense and that we cannot know God at all. Recognizing the distance, these miss the paradox of God's nearness, and they forget the power transforming our own limitations into prayer. They mistake darkness for absence, silence for nonexistence.

God is close within us, but also distant. He is familiar as friend, but also utterly beyond and other. We know and do not know. To forget either side of this pathway of our journey is to slide into one of the twin ditches of presumption or despair. And we must cling closely to the way now, for we walk unsteadily in darkness.

Listen carefully, and discern among the voices those which come from the Cherubim who stand balanced beside the Mercy Seat. One voice cries,

Hear, O Israel: The Lord our God is one Lord; and you shall love the Lord your God with all your hearts, and with all your soul, and with all your might. (Deut. 6:4, RSV)

And what is his name, the one God of our fathers?

God replied, "I am who am." Then he added, "This is what you shall tell the Israelites: I AM sent me to you." (Exod. 3:14.)

The other voice cries, "No one is good but God alone" (Mark 10:18; Luke 18:19). And what is his name? Jesus sends us forth "in the name of the Father, and of the Son, and of the holy Spirit" (Matt. 28:19).

Both voices speak together from the Cherubim, so that neither can be understood unless in counterpoint with the other. Because of our limits, we can listen closely to only one at a time—but remember that this is an artificial separation. Listening to one voice, always be conscious of the other.

But they speak only *words!* Weak words!

Words point the way. Cling to them, but follow their pointing in order to go beyond them. Rise, and do not be afraid.

3. Follow first the voice that names God "I AM." What does it mean to be?

We find ourselves touching again a point on our journey that we passed before. What does it mean *to be?* Why is there anything at all? Why among all possibilities for a universe has there emerged a place in which the likes of humankind might be drawn to wonder by the flash of a cardinal's wing on an ash bough?

Haven't we been here before? Are we traveling in circles? Perhaps our journey is like ascending a spiral staircase, where we pass the same point on the circle of human existence more than once, but always at a higher level, with deeper questions and richer insights.[1] The spiral of our journey is like the passing of the seasons, ever new yet ever the same.

Earlier we rejoiced in greeting the things of the world which emerge to meet us out of the power of God, which stand in beauty to reflect the wisdom of God, which reach in their interconnected destiny toward the goodness of God. Now we are called to peer into the darkness from which all emerges, gaze into the darkness toward which all reaches. Confidently we called it "God" before, filling in the darkness with whatever images or ideas of God our minds were able to project. Now, a little less naive because of our travels, we have to recognize that we may have underestimated the mystery of God. We may have overestimated the value of our images and ideas.

4. We stand alone in the Holy of Holies. Where we expected to meet God, we find silence, darkness. There is no thing there to touch us, no object to focus our thoughts, no other being facing us as another human person does. Where, then, *is* this God-being whom we have been so earnestly seeking?

Images and ideas crowd again into our mind, trying to shield us mercifully from the darkness. But for every image seen or dreamt, and for every idea perceived or thought, there is always the darkness from which it approaches us, the darkness into which it withdraws. Every thought and thing and person in our awareness hovers in that balance. How readily we cling to the thought and the thing, standing over against us as a familiar, comforting object. Yes, that tree is; I can see it! This mower is; I can feel it vibrating in my hands! But what does that is mean? Too readily we forget the balance of darkness that gives us the thought and the thing, the balance of darkness into which thoughts and things recede, the balance of darkness in which we ourselves stand as persons—so close to us that we cannot see it.

Bonaventure says, look how we fail to see the pure light by which we see every object that we see. Were a beam of pure light to be passing through this dark place, we would be able to see only the specks of dust that happened to be caught by it, or some object or other which the beam happened to touch. The pure light itself? "When the eye sees pure light, it seems to itself to see nothing" (5:4).

5. What then is the shape of this darkness which is no thing?

When we passed this way earlier, lower on the spiral staircase of our journey, we saw every object against the background of its surrounding setting, a setting which reaches out to a horizon and even beyond any horizon. Now we have to concentrate our mind on that horizon and beyond it, beyond any object. It isn't easy. It is like trying to focus on one's peripheral vision: Focusing makes it nonperipheral, and we lose the horizon in mere objects. It is like trying to gaze directly (without the aid of a mirror) into the eye which is gazing!

This is ridiculous! What does this confusing abstraction have to do with the real world and real people? What good is this dark Holy of Holies stuff, anyway! Give us the good old common-sense everyday world! Like this mower vibrating in my hands. And this tree. And the greening valley beyond it. And the roofs and trees and towers that mark the horizon. And beyond the horizon . . .

There it is again. Inescapable, the darkness is beyond the horizon. At this stage of our journey we can't ignore it any more. The darkness always gives forth whatever we see, always beckons as it withdraws beyond any limits.

I focus my gaze on the ash tree, but try to sensitize the edges of my mind to be conscious of the darkness, just as long ago we had to sensitize our body to be aware of something so simple and close to us as the air passing through our nostrils. Try it again: focus on an object, preferably a living thing rooted in the earth.

My ash tree has changed since we last attended to it. Its setting has been transformed from grays to greens. The horizon is not stark white against the cold blue of sky, but multicolored against puffy spring clouds and the blue beyond them.

And beyond the blue is the unchanging, ever-present darkness out of which all is coming to us, into which everything recedes from us. The tree's simple presence is revealed as a hovering balance, constantly emerging from darkness to meet me and constantly withdrawing from me into darkness.

The darkness is constant among change. No thing itself, it is the background of all awareness. Time itself is the pattern of this constancy: a pattern of flowing balance as all seems to emerge from darkness and withdraw again into it. But the darkness itself is timeless, beyond time. Tree, valley and I myself are all changeable, vulnerable—but the darkness remains. Horizons are linked into one by the surrounding darkness, so that the sense of unity and harmony that we found arising from the partnership of mind and world, is itself held together by the common emerging of all from the darkness, the common withdrawing of all into darkness. The darkness gives; the darkness beckons.

6. We have arrived at the root and core of our consciousness, the constant ground of every perception, image and thought.

So where are we, then?

Alone we stand in the Holy of Holies, balanced upon the giving and beckoning flow of darkness.

Alone.

Where then is God? After all this, are we left abandoned? Have we gone too far, and lost God?

> Where can I go from your spirit?
>   from your presence where can I flee?
> If I go up to the heavens, you are there;
>   if I sink to the nether world, you are present there.
> If I take the wings of the dawn,
>   if I settle at the farthest limits of the sea,
> Even there your hand shall guide me,
>   and your right hand hold me fast.
> If I say, "Surely the darkness shall hide me,
>   and night shall be my light"—
> For you darkness itself is not dark,
>   and night shines as the day.
> [Darkness and light are the same.]
> (Ps. 139:7–12)

Balanced in the glowing darkness, receiving its constant gift and responding to its constant beckoning, our being itself reaches out to *name* the one that gives, the one that beckons.

> Thee, God, I come from, to thee go,
> All day long I like a fountain flow
> from thy hand out, swayed about
> Mote-like in thy mighty glow.
> (Gerard Manley Hopkins)[2]

Beyond the darkness: God! Source of all giving: God! Goal of all beckoning: God! Ground of the whole whirling balance of our being: God!

But to call out is not to know, and the name is not the mystery. In the Holy of Holies, with awe we hear from the darkness: "Hear, O Israel: The Lord our God is one Lord; and you shall love the Lord your God ..." (Deut. 6:4, RSV). Responding only with bare, bright faith, we proclaim into the darkness: WE BELIEVE IN ONE GOD ...

7. Yet it is *words* that we hear, mere *words* that we proclaim! Words that fall clattering down the hard stone steps away from mystery and into the merely sensible, into what can be taken for granted. And such words as these, if they are proclaimed apart from the mystery, are hollow! ludicrous! hypocritical! blasphemous! (but inevitable, comical, forgivable).

God laughs.

Brother Bonaventure, you didn't warn us about the *pain* of this stage of the journey! Every name is a misnomer! Every revelation is a veil! Every understanding is a misunderstanding!

Look what has happened to our words and ideas! God is in all things but wholly beyond all things. The ground of all our being is nothing. The passing of time is the *constant* factor in consciousness. Source and goal are the same. The highest knowledge is to know that we do not know. True words mean more than they can say, and words that mean exactly what they say are false and misleading.

At this stage of our journey, common sense is set adrift. Incommensurables become equal, as if one constantly did calculations dividing by zero. Opposites which should conflict—like timelessness and the present, simplicity and complexity, constancy and change, unity and multiplicity, darkness and light—rather coincide! Now such contraries are true only when matched together, each balanced by its opposite. Clear and distinct ideas are proven unreal, truisms are false, logical axioms beg the question. Have we become befuddled in the darkness?

8. Rather, have we finally come to be able to see by the light of the infinity of God? "For you darkness itself is not dark, and night shines as the day" (Ps. 139:12). Is this darkness indeed "the supreme illumination of our mind" (5:4)?

Rich voices from the Cherubim say Yes, Yes, oh Yes. Using simple geometric figures, the voices illustrate what must happen in our mind if we are to think in the light of the infinity of God. What becomes of the clear, logical rules for a triangle, with its proportional three sides and 180-degree sum of angles, when the triangle is infinite? All sides coincide! No sides touch! And a circle? Circumference, diameter and center all coincide; the circumference is a straight line.[3] Bonaventure links space and time in another image:

> Because it [Being that is God] is eternal and most present,
> it therefore encompasses and enters all duration
> as if it were at one and the same time
> its center and circumference.
> . . . totally within all things and totally outside them
> [it] thus "is an intelligible sphere
> whose center is everywhere
> and whose circumference is nowhere." (5:8)[4]

The root and core of our consciousness, within us, coincides with the reality of God, beyond us. (Atman is Brahman, says the Hindu.) And nothing matters but God, beyond! (There is no God but God!) But in this Way of Heaven, everything present matters most deeply and truly. And of this God what can we say? It is not enough merely to say he exists; to say that he does not exist is obviously false. Both exists and not exists? No. Neither exists nor not exists? With the Buddhist approaching nirvana, we meet what is no thing—that mystery into which our paltry word "God" points.

What a tangled net words are! What a deceptive thing logic is! What oxlike stubbornness in the neat little dualities of true/false, yes/no! Here in the Holy of Holies, the luminous darkness responds to us again with silence. And our response?

> But the LORD is in his holy temple;
> silence before him, all the earth!
> (Hab. 2:20)

6

The Good God

This chapter leads us into contemplating God as Trinity,
focusing on the divine Good.

1. Is there yet *more*, beyond the luminous darkness of divine Being?
Beyond the silence? There is more. Within and beyond the darkness; above and beyond the silence.

Yet we remain in our ordinary place in this journey, continuing
to do our ordinary things. It is another weekend for me, one
without a list of things I must do! (Other than write.) There is time
to wander about the garden. Roses are in fragrant bloom now. Tiny
tomatoes have formed at the root of their wrinkled yellow blossoms.
Dark green thimbles hidden here and there mark sweet peppers
to come. The warm and fruitful breeze whispers promises that are
well on the way toward being fulfilled.

The sound of a gentle breeze—like Elijah we can hear in it the
summons to step forth and meet God (see 1 Kings 19:12–13, JB). The
voice from the Cherubim now cries, "No one is good but God alone"
(Mark 10:18). And our journey turns to respond to this voice.

At the same time, we need to recall constantly the voice to which
we responded in the previous stage of our journey, so that the two
voices are always balancing one with the other. The voice that spoke
of God as Being called us to recognize the dark silence of God's
transcendence, beyond time, beyond limit, beyond reason and
comprehension. The voice that now speaks of God as Good calls
us to recognize the bright radiance of God's sending himself forth
and embracing us, catching us up in realization, and returning us
to himself.

Again, we struggle with words. We have to: how else can we share
any insight at all? But now hear the words as coming forth out of
the silence. Do not be deceived into thinking that we understand;
the words mean far more than they can say. Words are like a finger
pointing: rather than concentrating on the finger, we must follow
the pointing beyond, into the luminous darkness of God.

2. *Good.* What does that word mean?

No, don't go to a dictionary; you'll just be confused. Try turning to the Psalms.

> Good and upright is the LORD;
>   thus he shows sinners the way.
> He guides the humble to justice,
>   he teaches the humble his way.
> (Ps. 25:8–9)
> Taste and see how good the LORD is;
>   happy the man who takes refuge in him.
> (Ps. 34:9)
> Gladden the soul of your servant,
>   for to you, O Lord, I lift up my soul;
> For you, O Lord, are good and forgiving,
>   abounding in kindness to all who call upon you.
> (Ps. 86:4–5)
> Sing joyfully to the LORD, all you lands;
>   serve the Lord with gladness;
>   come before him with joyful song . . .
> Give thanks to him; bless his name, for he is good:
>   the LORD, whose kindness endures forever,
>   and his faithfulness, to all generations.
> (Ps. 100:1, 4–5)
> Give thanks to the LORD, for he is good,
>   for his kindness endures forever.
> (Ps. 106:1)
> Praise the LORD, for the LORD is good;
>   sing praise to his name, which we love.
> (Ps. 135:3)

So sing the Psalms about God as Good.

If we probe what the word *good* here points toward, a threefold pattern stands out. First and most constant is the loving kindness of God as he generously sends himself forth to his people, giving himself to all who call upon him. Second is the uprightess of God, leading the humble in the right path toward himself. Third is the delight in the Lord—"taste and see!"—that evokes joyful praise.

The risk here is that we hear these words as if they referred to a mere man—a celestial *king*, of course, but *a mere being* up there in the sky that likes us, guides us and promises us a heaven of reward. Our childish images of God keep imposing themselves, and we forget the darkness. How shall we hear, then, these words that point into and beyond the darkness toward a Good that is no thing?

Listen to the first phase of the pattern: Good sending itself forth, like a fountain spraying outward or a light radiating brightness everywhere. But this overflowing good is God beyond limit, radiating *infinite* fullness.

What is that very fullness of God that is radiated forth?

God! God sending forth and sent; radiating and radiated, giving and given!

And between? Steadfast love is at the core of God's self-giving. Loving kindness is the root of the given. *Love* then is the eternal "between" in this relation beyond any thing and beyond all limit.

What name points into this mystery? "The name of the Father, and of the Son, and of the holy Spirit" (Matt. 28:19).

Trinity!

3. Don't think that we have arrived at something comfortably familiar! Some of us still recall from the memorized catechism "the mystery of three divine persons in one divine nature." We thought we knew something! Such poor, laughable fools we are.

We have seen in the darkness that the highest knowledge is to know that we do not know. (And yet we continue to speak, and we *should* continue!) Common sense was set adrift then. But *now*—now our words mock us (while still revealing). The drift races us over a waterfall!

For there in the unity of God beyond limit (and so beyond parts, or differences, or otherness: "one without a second," as the Upanishads say), there we find distinct persons in a mutual relationship! And this is *beyond* and within the transcendent unity of God. Inconceivable!—and so a scandal to those who believe that "There is no God but God."

And there in the eternity of God beyond limit (and so beyond change, or movement, or activity), there we find the radiant dynamism of sending, being sent, and union. And this is *beyond* and within the transcendent eternity of God! Inconceivable!—and so a scandal to those who think God must only be Unchanging Absolute.

Still we stand in the Holy of Holies, balanced in the luminous darkness. Unity and eternity we have heard in the silence, spoken by the first of the Cherubim. Trinity and dynamism we hear now from the second of the Cherubim. Trying to contemplate each voice has strained the mind. Words stretch their bonds.

Now—try to contemplate both together! Bonaventure says, "When you compare them with one another, you have reason to be lifted up to the highest wonder" (6:3).

The highest wonder: Words explode! They serve only to launch the mind above itself, beyond itself. *And yet there is more!*

4. After all, we have touched only the first phase of the pattern

of Good that we saw in the Psalms: the loving kindness of God giving himself forth. There is more. There is yet the right path for the humble. There is yet the delight and joyful praise. Trinity, after all, is a "mystery of *salvation*"—*we* are involved in Trinity!

The voices of the Cherubim between them bring us back to contemplate the overflowing emptiness of the Mercy Seat above the Ark, where the mystery of God dwells *near to us.* The voices combine in counterpoint, in harmony that is more than their sum. For it has pleased God that Trinity itself should explode outward, radiating outward in the name of the Father into a world that reveals God in the name of the Son, and that is drawn to return to union with God in the name of the holy Spirit.

Again, only at a higher level, we find ourselves caught up in this cosmic embrace of Trinity—one and manifold, transcendent and near, eternal and dynamic. We shudder in wonder. But we have not yet reached the highest revelation. "Now this is eternal life, that they should know you, the only true God, and the one whom you sent, Jesus Christ" (John 17:3). Jesus Christ: one in being with the Father in divinity; one in being with us in our humanity. Divine Word from within and beyond the luminous darkness, become a human being—*flesh!* just as we are.

Impossible! Absurd! Scandalous! Blasphemous!

Only if your narrow logic has not yet been exploded; only if your common sense has not yet drifted to the waterfall.

Jesus Christ. Astonishing!

5. So easily we forget to be astonished. Jesus has become so easy to take for granted. Habit has allowed us to speak too glibly of this man as Son of God. We need to remember the scandal of Jesus.

He was, after all, a man. He lived a very ordinary life in an unimportant but pesky province of the Roman Empire. You could not have picked him out in a crowd of dusty young Jewish men of the time—until he started saying startling things and doing astonishing works. Then you could pick him out: That's him—the bloody mess there hanging from the middle cross.

> There was in him no stately bearing to make us look at him, nor appearance that would attract us to him. (Isaiah 53:2)

This is the Son of God? You've got to be kidding! This is the revelation of the Father? What, did we come in late and miss the punch line?

Jesus said, "The Father and I are one! . . . Believe the works, so that you may realize [and understand] that the Father is in me and

I am in the Father" (John 10: 30, 38). The first voice from the Cherubim interprets for us: Jesus was saying that the mystery of God beyond every thing, beyond the darkness—the mystery of God that transcends our words, our images, time itself—this mystery is right here, an ordinary man *in the flesh*, and talking with us in ordinary words! (Well, maybe in *extraordinary* words, but words nonetheless.) And this man emptied himself into the degradation of the cross in order to reveal that mystery to us.

This we can take for granted?

When Jesus said such things, his closest disciples did *not* take him for granted. They missed the entire point!

> "I am the way and the truth and the life. No one comes to the Father except through me. If you know me, then you will also know my Father. From now on you do know him and have seen him."
>
> Philip said to him, "Master, show us the Father, and that will be enough for us." [gasp!]
>
> Jesus said to him, "Have I been with you for so long a time and you still do not know me, Philip? Whoever has seen me has seen the Father. How can you say, 'Show us the Father'? Do you not believe that I am in the Father and the Father is in me? (John 14:6–10)

Poor Philip! The Gospel itself seems to mock the disciples, but it does so for a purpose. The folly of Philip stands as a warning to all of us: do not forget to be astonished at *the man* Jesus Christ!

6. The scandal of Jesus Christ extends further. The second voice from the Cherubim reminds us how in Trinity God sends himself forth and embraces us, catches us up in the way of realization, and returns us to himself. We have seen that Jesus is the one sent forth to reveal the Father. Jesus is the way and the truth and the life. By abiding in Jesus we know God and return to union with God. But where is Jesus now? Where is the Father revealed, the way shown, the joyful union attained?

He's in heaven now, of course. What a relief! The scandal of the *flesh* is removed, and we comfortably imagine a divine, disembodied Jesus. No need to be astonished any more. We're free to worship "spiritually."

Wait. That is not what Jesus said. (Be ready for astonishment at an even greater scandal!)

Look at the foolish Philip as the model of the unlikely and inadequate people who were disciples to Jesus. It was of *these* that Jesus said to the Father, "As you sent me into the world, so I sent them into the world" (John 17:18). As the Father sent Jesus, so Jesus sends Philip and company. *They* are the ones sent forth to reveal

Jesus. *They* are the way to Jesus as the truth and the life. By abiding with *them* one abides in Jesus and knows God.

This unlikely crew? He can't really mean *that*!

No? Hold on—he meant much more:

> "I pray not only for them, but also for those who will believe in me through their word, so that they may all be one, as you, Father, are in me and I in you, that they also may be in us, that the world may believe that you sent me."(John 17:20–21)

Those who will believe: that's *us*. That they may be one—as one with Jesus as Jesus is one with the Father? US? IMPOSSIBLE!

At least make it that our best inner, spiritual selves cleave longingly to God in prayer, or that the pure inner core of our spirits touches God (as Atman is Brahman to the Hindu). That would be less a scandal!

But that would not be what Jesus said. He said US! in the flesh! "Warts and all!" Us in all of our confusion and spiritual ambiguity and misunderstanding and failure. In our fleshly bodies, for heaven's sake! Us as his people gathered: church. Us as his people simply living together: family. Us.

Astonishing! WE are the Mercy Seat! WE are the place where God dwells upon the earth!

7. Bonaventure says, "In this consideration is the perfection of the mind's illumination" (6:7). We near the end of our journey.

After all of our struggling and climbing on this journey, after even arriving at the Holy of Holies in the temple atop the Mountain of God, after probing the divine darkness and being swept up into the saving whirlwind of Trinity, after all this we are shocked to find ourselves standing now in an ordinary Sunday church among ordinary people gathered around the table of the Eucharist. After all this we find ourselves now in our ordinary homes gathered with our families to share our common meals. So we have arrived into our ordinariness, blinking in astonishment.

We have arrived, in the sixth stage of our journey, at the meaning of the sixth day of creation: Then God said: "Let us make man in our image, after our likeness" (Gen. 1:26). The dark mystery of God beyond every thing, the mystery that transcends our words, our images, and time itself—that mystery *is happening* here and now, constantly, in every detail of our ordinariness. The radiant mystery of God sending himself forth and embracing us, catching us up in the way of realization, and returning us to himself—this mystery *is at play* among us, in our sharings and our follies at every moment.

As we stand of a Sunday as church to share the bread and the cup, ALL THIS IS HAPPENING! Incredible.

It's words, though. It's still all words, unexploded words. We're still just thinking, meditating. The reality hasn't hit yet. Perhaps that's a kindness.

Supposing, though, that all these words were to explode with that meaning beyond what they can say . . . Supposing we were to *see*, really, what is actually happening as the mystery of God plays among us . . . Suddenly in the middle of an ordinary Sunday congregation, we might cry out, wordless, in a joyous agony of wonder! Heads would turn. Eyes would pop. Wouldn't that be a scandal!

Rest

Here our journey opens upward, beyond itself;
we come to peace and rest; we pass over into God.

1. It was a pure, simple joy to harvest the first tomato of the season. Feeling the warm, slow breeze and the earthy stickiness of tomato greens, I carefully twisted it loose. Evenly red, round and juicy: a triumph. With the garden's lettuce, broccoli and chives (the peppers aren't quite ready yet), my family can celebrate summer with a salad.

So it is time for our efforts to come to fruit. Such a journey we have traveled together! In six steps we have climbed the throne of wisdom with Solomon. Six days of creation have passed, and now we enter the seventh day of rest. With Moses we have struggled from Egypt to the mountain of God and climbed into the dark fire at its peak. With Isaiah we have found ourselves astonished and unworthy before the throne of God, and we have sensed God reaching toward us in the burning, healing power of the six-winged Seraph.

With Peter and James and John we have followed Jesus up the mountain of transfiguration. Lord, it is good that we are here! Now, please, can we camp? (See Matt. 17:4.) We're exhausted: is it finally time to rest? (See Luke 9:32.) Is it time for peace at last?

> "Peace I leave with you;
> my peace I give to you.
> Not as the world gives do I give it to you.
> Do not let your hearts be troubled or afraid."
> (John 14:27)

Peace and rest "not as the world gives"? Not then the rest of sleep; not a peace of repose. What kind of peace, then? What kind of rest?

Can you remember learning to ride a bicycle? Fear and struggle and scrapes and bruises—and Daddy's hand firm on the wobbling thing—until a moment that happened so simply that we didn't recognize it right away. Astonished, we found ourselves in balance! We were riding free! It was as if we had learned to fly.

The rest at our journey's end is like resting in that balance: dynamic but still, fear gone; the wobbling, worried effort transformed into ease. And once we found that balance, however many years passed with forgetfulness, it has always been there within us to find again.

All our journey has led us up to this peace and this rest. We have sought God in the beauty of the world around us. We have found his traces in the partnership of mind and world that happens in our every perception. We have seen the vestige of Trinity in the shape of our efforts and our commitments. We have discovered the divine image in our own being called into God in spite of ourselves. We have probed the silence of divine darkness, and we have been caught up in the saving whirlwind of Trinity. We began with Jesus, followed Jesus as the Way, and arrived at Jesus embodied (incredibly!) in our ordinariness as church and as family.

But even now we are still just thinking and using images and words, still wobbling. We are called to pass over, through, beyond.

Rise, and do not be afraid.

How are we to attain this passing over, and so arrive at peace and rest? It will be given to us. Simply, in a moment we might not recognize right away. In the midst of all the words and images that speak of God and point to God and tell us of being caught up in God, by grace there will come a moment when effort and struggle cease, words and images burst open, and the balance comes. There will be a moment of simple recognition.

This is *real. He is really there.* No thunder crash or trumpet flash. Simple as a gentle breeze. Oh. Yes. My Lord and my God! (John 20:28). Of course! (But how utterly astonishing!)

Then everything will be different (but with no perceptible change):

> I have dealt with great things that I do not understand;
> things too wonderful for me, which I cannot know.
> I had heard of you by word of mouth,
> but now my eye has seen you.
> Therefore I disown what I have said,
> and repent in dust and ashes.
> (Job 42:3–6)

God laughs! and we laugh with him and in him.

2. In the midst of the Mercy Seat—in the midst of ourselves—we find Jesus Christ, the Crucified.

Perhaps now we can understand, and say with Paul:

> I have been crucified with Christ; yet I live, no longer I, but Christ lives in me; insofar as I now live in the flesh, I live by faith in the Son of God who has loved me and given himself up for me. (Gal. 2:19–20).

No longer I . . .

In that moment of recognition, all the wobbling worry of "I" (I can't do it! I'm out of control! Stop! I need to keep my feet down! Yiyee!)— poof, gone like mist in sunlight. Instead? Christ lives in us, among us. So simple; so astonishing.

Instead of the muck of "I" so full of failure and ambiguity, there is Christ and the Easter power of God transforming:

> If the Spirit of the one who raised Jesus from the dead dwells in you, the one who raised Christ from the dead will give life to your mortal bodies also, through his Spirit that dwells in you. (Rom. 8:11)

Peace and rest then are away from the worry over self. Peace and rest are in the balance of this real, tangible faith.

> What will separate us from the love of Christ? Will anguish, or distress, or persecution, or famine, or nakedness, or peril, or the sword? . . . For I am convinced . . . nor height, nor depth, nor any other creature will be able to separate us from the love of God in Christ Jesus our Lord. (Rom. 8:35, 38–39).

We have known this all along, haven't we? Already in these words, in an earlier circle of our journey, we have found the strength to go on in spite of ourselves. Now we find in them a simple statement of what is happening in us: one with Jesus, one in God.

Now my eye has seen you!

3. Is this what Francis saw? Brother Bonaventure, as you climbed the mountain Alverno to find a way to follow Francis, you were in the very spot where the six-winged Seraph appeared to Francis and burned into his body the marks of the crucified Jesus. Can we now recognize, in Francis's moment of ecstacy, what was happening?

The story is told that faithful Brother Leo, worried about Francis, sought him out on the mountain. He discovered Francis caught up in astonished prayer: "Who are you, my dearest God? and what am I, your vilest little worm and useless little servant?"[1]

This is *real.* God is really here. In spite of the "I"! So simple; so astonishing.

We can let go, then, as Francis did. Pass over out of ourselves, and let ourselves be caught up in the simple recognition of who God is! Nothing matters but God!

4. Words have exploded. Common sense has been overthrown, launched upwards beyond itself. Thought tangles unless it transcends itself, opening upward.

Driven (called?) by unsought destiny, we have struggled on our journey with words and images and thoughts. Following them as they pointed beyond themselves, we have desired the reality of God and waited for the gift of God. Now dump the words! Scrap the thought! Pierce through the images! Now is only simple recognition and wordless response.

> We speak God's wisdom, mysterious, hidden, which God
> predetermined before the ages for our glory. . . .
>> "What eye has not seen, and ear has not heard,
>> and what has not entered the human heart,
>> what God has prepared for those who love him,"
> this God has revealed to us through the Spirit. (1 Cor. 2:7, 9–10)

5. Now everything that we have done—all our efforts and achievements, however indispensable they may have been along our journey—becomes laughable.

With Moses we stand on the mountaintop, with all left behind. Shall we find rest? The Lord said, " My presence will go with you, and I will give you rest" (Exod. 33:14, RSV).

Rest in the presence of God; rest in the going rather than in repose. What is that like? Moses wondered that, too, and said, "Do let me see your glory!" (Exod. 33:18). Like Moses we ask with childish eagerness for what is so far beyond us that we cannot even begin to fathom the distance. But God kindly shelters us as he did Moses.

> "When my glory passes I will set you in the hollow of the rock and
> will cover you with my hand until I have passed by. Then I will
> remove my hand, so that you may see my back; but my face is not to
> be seen." (Exod. 33:22–23).

"You may see my *back*"? What does that mean?

A voice from the Cherubim sings that the spirit which has become free "rises ever higher and will always make its flight yet higher."[2] Like Moses we are called to follow into God as God passes into his own infinity. Like Moses we are called to follow ceaselessly, eternally, to fly higher and infinitely higher in circles ever the same and ever new.

Why can no one see God's face and live ? The same voice answers, "He who thinks God is something to be known does not have life."[3] Our rest is in this unknowing.

At the destination of the journey, our rest is in the destiny to follow endlessly, eternally, into God. Our rest is to rise infinitely higher into God. Our journey is into God himself! Of course there is no end! Let go. Rise, and do not be afraid.

> For transcending yourself and all things,
> by the immeasurable and absolute ecstasy of a pure mind,

> leaving behind all things
> and freed from all things,
> you will ascend
> to the superessential ray
> of the divine darkness. (7:5)[4]

6. But how do we achieve this ? We don't; it is given.

Turn to prayer, wordless prayer. Shed the baggage of words and thinking. Free yourself for the gift and the surprise. Let go, let your feet leave the ground. Be carried into the brilliant darkness.

Rise, and do not be afraid. Spread arms, spread wings—you can fly.

> You have seen for yourselves . . . how I bore you up on eagle wings and brought you here to myself. (Exod. 19:4)

(Arms spread like the cross, wings spread like the Seraph—with Christ *fly* within yourself, outside yourself, beyond yourself.)

> For if we have grown into union with him through a death like his, we shall also be united with him in the resurrection. . . . If, then, we have died with Christ, we believe that we shall also live with him. (Rom. 6:5, 8)

Our rest is the balance of death and resurrection, like the eagle soaring high and hovering in the gentle breeze.

> They that hope in the LORD will renew their strength,
> they will soar as with eagles' wings;
> They will run and not grow weary,
> walk and not grow faint.
> (Isa. 40:31)

Walk? Run? Again? Haven't we finished our journey? We have. We have arrived at the beginning.

Here ends the soul's journey into God ...

Back to Earth

In this chapter we descend from the mountain
and enter again the life of routine, of demands, of action—
which will never again be quite the same.

1. There is always more . . .

It is time to come down from the mountain, time to return to earth. Duties call; the garden needs tending.

The dry air is a little cooler these days as I write. The tired garden still presents its fruit: tomatoes a little woody now, broccoli and peppers smaller and tougher. The seasons turn; old tasks come undone and new tasks must be done. Here we go again, round and around.

It was autumn in 1259 when Bonaventure descended from Mount Alverno and returned to the tasks and the conflicts that overfilled his life. Immediately he got busy and wrote *The Soul's Journey,* and several other works as well. In the next year he had to struggle so that the young Franciscan Order could survive and grow. Within two years he faced an agonizing conflict: he had to pass harsh judgment on the man who had preceded him as head of the Order, a man now known as *Blessed* John of Parma. In these dilemmas, what assurance did he have that what he did was "the right thing"? None. In spiritual ambiguity, he had to act.

Francis himself descended from Alverno. Unable to walk because of the marks of the Crucified in his body, Francis went forth anyway on his mission, carried by his brothers. "Let us begin, brothers," he said, "to serve the Lord our God, for up to now we have hardly progressed."[1]

On our journey, we have arrived at the beginning. It is the eighth day: the last and the first, the day of transformation and renewal.

2. The exultation of our spiritual flight is past now. The joy of discovering the reality of God is fading. After the mountaintop comes the letdown. Is the spiritual journey after all just an episode in our busyness? Is it all over now, like a vacation trip surviving only in a stack of misplaced photos and in fading

memories? Or is something else happening in this stage of our journey?

After all, we *should* feel some sense of loss. It is only natural to want to settle on the mountaintop.

> "Lord, it is good that we are here. If you wish, I will make three tents here." (Matt. 17:4)

The taste of the Lord is good, but it would be a mistake to confuse the taste with the Lord. Spiritual flight is exhilarating, but it would be a mistake to glory in flight as an end in itself. Balancing in the luminous darkness at the core of consciousness is exalting, but it would be a mistake to rest in the balance and not follow its pointing into the one that gives, the one that beckons. It would be a worse mistake to fail to follow where he leads us.

It is a delusion to seek the height of spirituality as an end in itself. In that way the "I," which should have died along the way of our journey, resuscitates itself as some kind of horror-movie monster. "Even Satan masquerades as an angel of light" (2 Cor. 11:14). We have been called along the journey to the mountain of God. But we have not been called to stay there.

3. Then why *have* we been called there? What's the point? Why bother with all the struggle of this journey? To find out why, let's see from the Bible what happened in the lives of those who journeyed to meet God.

From the mountaintop of his meeting with God, the frightened Moses was sent down to rescue a poor band of people from the most powerful empire in the world. From the mountain meeting with God in the gentle breeze, the dejected Elijah was sent down to spark two political revolutions and to startle God's people back to faithfulness. From his heavenly vision, the overwhelmed Isaiah was sent down to point out God's way to his people—and to experience failure and frustration. From his meeting with God, the unlucky Jeremiah was sent down to confront the powers-that-be, to protest his king's policies, to suffer hostility and anger, and to fail. From the mountain of Jesus' ascension, the confused apostles had to turn to their task: "But you will receive power when the holy Spirit comes upon you, and you will be my witnesses in Jerusalem, throughout Judea and Samaria, and to the ends of the earth" (Acts 1:8).

No one called by God stays on the mountaintop. Everyone descends. Everyone returns to the ordinary world. With a mission.

4. Were we given a *mission* on our journey? We heard no voices commanding us to confront a Pharaoh. We were given no prophetic

message to deliver—and no divine assurance, either! Yet as we return from the mountaintop to our routine and to the demands upon us, things are not quite the same. Things will never be quite the same.

Once we have traveled this journey, everything in our world and work is now subject to judgment in relation to the way of God. What seemed important before, now recedes. What we may have overlooked before, now stands out. Further, everything is now touched by grace. What may have seemed impossible or impractical before, now seems clearly the thing to do. Where we felt weakness or indecision before, now we sense a power beyond our own.

Where in this is a prophetic mission? As we enter again upon our world and our work, we have to remember those things which we discovered on our journey. Then we will hear the command: Go, speak to this people. Gently confront these powers-that-be. Quietly bear witness, beginning at home, then in the circles around us, and even to the ends of the earth.

5. All right, then, what are those things we should remember from our journey? What are those things we should bear witness to?

Our journey awakened dimensions of world, mind and spirit which tend to be ignored in the world around us. (Everything opens upward, and outward!) Our habits of consciousness have changed, and our actions and words will witness to that.

The natural world around us has demanded that we recognize it as a precious gift not to be taken for granted. But that is not the way our society sees things. It is more likely that cost-efficiency and the maximization of profit determine how we treat the natural world. On our journey, we have learned to recognize that narrow attitude for what it is: vicious violence against the work of God. It is a *spiritual* crime that we are called like prophets to expose and to fight! (Yet to forgive and to heal.)

On our journey we found ourselves called not only to stewardship, but to praise. We are called to be the voice by which the earth praises God. Have we come then to recognize the immense prophetic importance of the artist, the poet, the musician and the dancer?

> Oh, that today you would hear his voice:
> "Harden not your hearts. . . . "
> (Ps. 95:7–8)

Our journey led us to recognize powerful mysteries at work in ourselves as human persons. Here is the manifestation of God, and here is the world's response to God: human persons in community.

Mindful of the meaning of human person and human community, we now reenter a hostile world. In this world, the body readily becomes an object of exploitation alienated from person. In this world, meaningful work is unavailable to many (it keeps costs down to have a labor surplus, they say). In this world, teamwork is often replaced by backstabbing competition. In this world, a love commitment might be abandoned if there is a pause in short-term satisfaction. In this world, learning becomes a mere commodity. God is clouded; the song of the earth is muted and goes sour. Into our mouths, in spite of ourselves, the words of the prophets will rise:

> Thus says the Lord:
> For three transgressions of Israel,
> and for four, I will not revoke the punishment;
> Because they sell the righteous for silver,
> and the needy for a pair of shoes—
> they that trample the heads of the poor into the dust of the earth,
> and turn aside the way of the afflicted. . . .
> (Amos 2:6–7, RSV).

Yet indignation, if indeed it is inspired, will be tempered by a simple and clear sense of what is truly important:

> You have been told, O man, what is good,
> and what the LORD requires of you:
> Only to do the right and to love goodness,
> and to walk humbly with your God.
> (Mic. 6:8)

After all, on our journey we have learned to be spiritually cautious. It was *before* his whirlwind meeting with God that Job said, "I hold fast my righteousness, and will not let it go" (Job 27:6, RSV). Harsh, righteous judgment smells too much of the muck of "I" and makes us accomplices of those who abuse the Bible as a hammer to pound on others.

We are where we are because God has brought us. We have no claim to pass judgment on others. If we have traveled this journey, we know well that anger at wrongs must be transformed into shared pain at common suffering, and into resolve toward change. Recognition of the shortcomings of others must be transformed into laughter and healing. Conflict must be transformed into creative, cooperative peace.

> Beloved,
> if God so loved us,

we also must love one another.
(1 John 4:11)

Well, then, it appears that we *have* been given a prophetic mission through our journey! We are sent as Jesus was sent—

> "The Spirit of the Lord is upon me,
> because he has anointed me
> to bring glad tidings to the poor.
> He has sent me to proclaim liberty to captives
> and recovery of sight to the blind,
> to let the oppressed go free,
> and to proclaim a year acceptable to the Lord.
> (Luke 4:18–19).

Us? *We* are sent to do all this?

Us. (Who else? We are the ones who have come to believe, and whom Jesus has sent forth.)

Here and now, in our ordinary families and churches and work and leisure, we are sent to *work* as well as to pray:

> Your kingdom come,
> your will be done,
> on earth as in heaven.
> (Matt. 6:10).

6. But how are we to carry out this mission? We have jobs, families to support, bills to pay! Who has time to be a hero like Moses or Elijah?

Who talks of heroism? No thunder-crash or earthquake is needed. It is the eighth day, the day of transformation and renewal. Transformation need not be violent:

"The kingdom of heaven is like yeast that a woman took and mixed with three measures of wheat flour until the whole batch was leavened." (Matt. 13:33)

Some of the most dramatic transformations in nature have been accomplished not by earthquake or volcano, but like the Grand Canyon by the slow and steady flow of so weak a thing as water.

> Nothing in the world
> is as soft and yielding as water.
> Yet for dissolving the hard and inflexible,
> Nothing can surpass it.
> The soft overcomes the hard;
> the gentle overcomes the rigid.
> Everyone knows this is true,
> but few can put it into practice.
> (*Tao te Ching*)[2]

Once we have traveled this journey, gentle changes should flow into our lives, forming simple but significant habits: what we choose to spend money on, what we choose to eat, what we invest time in, what motivates us to action or to anger, what we enjoy as leisure, how we vote. So the shape of our mission emerges: it is like what we plant in our garden and what we weed out. Companions on this journey, we together work softly and steadily "until the whole batch is leavened."

7. But, in all this work, how do we know we're right? We don't. Making this journey does not remove our spiritual ambiguity, nor does it guarantee wisdom. There is no assurance that we will succeed, either. In fact, failure is more likely. Ask Jeremiah!

There is no guarantee that we will even feel good about what we do. In fact, suffering is more likely.

> "Whoever wishes to come after me must deny himself, take up his cross, and follow me. For whoever wishes to save his life will lose it, but whoever loses his life for my sake will find it." (Matt. 16:24–25)

But in all this ambiguity, at least there is the supporting community of the church, the safe haven of God's people, right? Don't count on it. Once we have traveled this journey, the contrast is more evident between God's workings on the one hand and, on the other, uninspired or autocratic clergymen pandering to congregations desiring only complacency, routine and prejudice. The pain of that contrast is excruciating, sometimes almost unbearable. Sometimes it is the churches which make us feel most alone. Yet, given our spiritual ambiguity, who are we to pass judgment on the churches?

Then how on earth are we supposed to put the lessons of the journey into action? We can't be sure we're right. We don't see good results. We don't necessarily feel good. We're likely to be all alone out on a limb. Why try?

8.

> But the Lord answered me,
> Say not, "I am too young."
> To whomever I send you, you shall go;
> whatever I command you, you shall speak.
> Have no fear before them,
> because I am with you to deliver you, says the LORD.
> (Jer. 1:7–8).

To deliver us—even from our "I"? from our own ambiguity and mistakes and foolishness?

What, are we still worried about the "I"? If the "I" has died along our journey, we can find laughter in our mistakes and foolishness:

"We are fools on Christ's account" (1 Cor. 4:10). But there is no guarantee that the "I" has died. That is part of our foolishness. We can make no claim; we cannot even claim that we make no claim!

God laughs. The "I" dissolves in laughter.

With worry over the "I" out of the way, then we are freed to act in real love:

> Love is patient, love is kind. It is not jealous, [love] is not pompous, it is not inflated, it is not rude, it does not seek its own interests, it is not quick-tempered, it does not brood over injury, it does not rejoice over wrongdoing but rejoices with the truth. It bears all things, believes all things, hopes all things, endures all things. Love never fails. (1 Cor. 13:4–8)

How does this happen? Let go. Act without attachment. Act with self-forgetful love. Rise, and do not be afraid.

9. It is God who has called us, God who has sent us. It is for God to calculate the results and to estimate the worth. If we do what we can to plant the seeds of the Kingdom in our living and our working, then it is for God to cause the growth. If we do what we can to be leaven in the world, then our small and ambiguous efforts may be transformed by God just as the seed grows, just as bread brought in offering is transformed.

We are to work steadily and softly to plant in our lives the values of the Kingdom: the integrity of the earth; the dignity of human persons in body, in mind, in spirit and in community; justice; wisdom; peace. Don't expect to see sensational results. But act in hope, even in joy. Be open to grace. Be ready for the gift and the surprise.

> For after we have obeyed the Lord,
> and in His Spirit nurtured on earth
> the values of human dignity, brotherhood and freedom,
> and indeed all the good fruits
> of our nature and enterprise,
> we will find them again,
> but freed of stain, burnished and transfigured.
> This will be so when Christ hands over to the Father
> a kingdom eternal and universal:
> "a kingdom of truth and life
> of holiness and grace, of justice, love and peace."
> (Vatican II, *Gaudium et Spes* 39)[3]

10. So we have arrived at the beginning! Do you regret now that you have undertaken this journey? It demands more than we expected, doesn't it? And it ends not in a destination but in an ongoing destiny. But in the destiny itself there is rest for the weary

traveler, the rest of balance. After all, it is God who acts. It is the whirlwind of his saving power that we find ourselves caught up in, embraced by.

It is so easy to forget! Daily demands spin us about, and we lose our sense of direction. Hours and days disappear without a trace in our awareness. Then there are slack times, especially if we're laid off, or sick, or retired. Dry days disappear without accomplishment, and we endure the thirsty anguish of drifting. In the whirl or in the drift, a cry of sorrow and frustration and longing builds within us.

Prayer; wordless prayer. Recognize it for what it is.

Remember to return, snatching what moments you can find or make. Return and find again that little place of quiet where you can retreat within yourself. Find again that point of rest within you that is like balancing on a bicycle (like the gliding of an eagle!). You have found it on the journey. Once you have found it, it is always there hidden within you to find again, and again, and again. Rise, and do not be afraid.

Well, then, let us be on our way! The spiral staircase of our journey opens above and ahead, like the turning of seasons always the same and always new. The flight of the eagle soars higher still. Rise, and do not be afraid.

By the way, have you noticed the company with whom we travel? By our journey, we are joined together with Mary, the apostles and martyrs, and all the saints. And with each other.

Our journey is ended. Let us go forth to love and serve the Lord. Thanks be to God!

Incipit speculatio pauperis in deserto.
(Here begins the reflection of the poor man in the desert . . .)

LIGNUM VITAE

THE TREE OF LIFE

Introduction

While *The Soul's Journey* describes a spiritual ascent that is principally an intellectual quest, *The Tree of Life* is a reflection on prayer
that focuses more concretely on Jesus as the Bible presents him.
While *The Soul's Journey* meditates on levels of experience and
awareness, *The Tree of Life* meditates principally upon *texts*: passages
and stories from the Bible.

This part of *A Retreat with St. Bonaventure* is a set of meditations
upon a very terse but suggestive work of Bonaventure. It follows
that work's suggestions, again from the point of view of a twentieth-
century Catholic layperson.

Bonaventure's text is terse, providing just a morsel for meditation. This writing expands into meditation not only on Bonaventure's text but on the Biblical inspiration for each of his passages.
And yet in its terseness, each of Bonaventure's passages points in
many directions, directions evident in relation to the whole of
Bonaventure's writings. This writing selects among those directions
for points to develop.

This part of *A Retreat with St. Bonaventure* is *not* then a meditation
on Bonaventure's text, as if the reader is invited to meditate upon
Bonaventure meditating on the Gospel stories. It is an attempt to
go *with* Bonaventure through the way of the Tree of Life. First we
seek a spiritual empathy with Bonaventure, to appreciate his insight
as if from within. Then, *with* Bonaventure, we look upon the same
mysteries of the Gospel that he did, guided by him but not focused
on him.

Therefore this writing is modeled as a dialogue. Bonaventure's
work uses the device of the "dialogue with the soul." This writing
adds a twentieth-century companion to Bonaventure in a kind of
Socratic dialogue—but the companion is a little less naive than
Socrates' typical interlocutor.

This reflection on *The Tree of Life* should *follow* the reflections on
The Soul's Journey in the first part of this book. While it might seem
sensible to *start* with familiar passages from the Bible, rather than

with the philosophical considerations of *The Soul's Journey*, this reflection assumes that the reader has already developed some spiritual empathy with Bonaventure and some understanding of his spiritual vision. Here the reader is invited to *be* Bonaventure's companion along this way.

Readers should again be tempted to seek out Bonaventure's text, for this reflection follows Bonaventure's, section by numbered section. Further, readers may want to have a Bible handy to ensure that the stories for each section are fresh in their minds before they join Bonaventure in reflection.

Prologue

I have been crucified with Christ;
yet I live,
no longer I,
but Christ lives in me.
(Galatians 2:19–20)

1. This is the whole point, Bonaventure says. This is what the Christian life is all about.

Are you saying then, Brother Bonaventure, that if I wish to worship God truly and become a true disciple of Christ, then those words of Paul must become my own? It's that simple?

Is it so simple a thing to make those words your own?

Oh, it is simple to mouth and memorize them. I can even feel a momentary emotional thrill, a kind of prayerful sweetness, as I read or hear them. So reassuring such a feeling is—I can look at myself and see how holy I am, how devout.

How phony.

True. So that's not what you mean, is it, Brother Bonaventure?

No. What I mean is that Christ and his cross have to become such a part of you, you such a part of Christ and his cross, that . . . there is no more "I."

How can I accomplish such a thing?

Accomplish? Such a thing as this is not an accomplishment or an achievement. It comes as a gift. It simply happens.

Oh, that's right.

But it does not come without your seeking.

Huh? How do I *seek* for something surprising to *happen* to me?

The seeking itself is a gift. It chooses you. It happens, arousing and drawing you rather than merely being your own initiative. It is as absorbing and fascinating and as simple as . . . falling in love.

> On my bed at night I sought him whom my heart loves—
> I sought him but I did not find him. . . .
> I adjure you, daughters of Jerusalem,
> by the gazelles and hinds of the field,

Do not arouse, do not stir up love
before its own time.
(Song of Songs 3:1, 5)

You surprise me, Brother Bonaventure! I thought you spent your life in a cloister. Yet you speak of falling in love? I must say, Brother Bonaventure, that I have been puzzled that you quote the Old Testament's marvelously erotic love song more often than any of its other books. Is this why? Is it because seeking Christ is so much like young love?

Yes, it is. Rather than concentrating to remember my beloved's image, I am haunted by it; rather than carefully reasoning, I am obsessed; rather than choosing, I am caught up beyond myself. I might do foolish things. I am no longer quite myself. It can actually be rather embarrassing, even in a cloister.

Really? Then that's what real prayer must be like, right? Not pious efforts or righteous routines—it's simple and crazy, like falling in love.

Something like that. All longing and flowers at first, maybe. And then it grows, as the flowers fade, into the patient, close engendering of fruit.

Until I can truly say, "I have been crucified with Christ."

The cross then must become intimate to your life—as close as love, worn as a lover's locket:

My beloved is to me a bag of myrrh,
that lies between my breasts.
(Song of Songs 1:13, RSV)

2. How is the cross of Christ to become so intimate to my life, Brother Bonaventure? How am I to become so close to Christ that Paul's words may become my own?

Look to the Gospels: seek Christ there, and the gift will come. Like a young lover, walk the street where Christ lives—hoping that by chance you will really meet him, hoping that it will happen.

But I've read the Gospels and the earth didn't move. I've even studied the Gospels, guided by historians and archeologists, and the pavement stays firmly beneath my feet.

You have to *pray* the Gospels. You have to *hear* the Good News simply and from the heart.

Oh, I've heard that before! Seven centuries of self-righteous Bible-thumpers have used that line in order to prevent people from thinking. And then they have twisted the Scriptures in order to make money or to build up their power or even to turn people to hatred and murder! No, modern approaches to Scripture study are a real blessing! They help to expose the frauds who read their own agenda into the Bible instead of letting the Bible speak on its own terms. Shakespeare was right: even the devil can quote Scripture to his purpose! Don't you tell me to go back to naive literalism!

I think you may protest too much. Are you perhaps a little like a person who has been abused and so is afraid of love? Think, now. Did I ask you to abandon anything that your modern Scripture study has gained? And honestly, have you really been able to hear the Good News simply and from the heart?

No. I'm still really . . . untouched. Christ and his cross are still . . . an abstraction, like a romantic fantasy. I guess maybe I have missed something, Brother Bonaventure. How can I learn to pray the Gospel?

That's better. First, take the Gospel stories simply, just as they are. (You may want to hold your modern study ready in the background, though. You'll want to notice if anyone makes foolish or fraudulent claims.) Take the story and then enter imaginatively into it. Touch it and let it touch you as if you were present there in first-century Palestine with Jesus and his followers. Try to breathe the air that they breathe, there by the Sea of Galilee. Try to see and hear Jesus as he speaks or acts. Notice how the people around him respond, and try to feel what they are feeling. Get to know the personalities of the apostles. And get to know Jesus as the people around knew him.

Okay, I'm willing to try if you'll show me how. But how can doing that make it happen? There has to be something more.

There is. As you enter imaginatively into the Gospel stories, old familiar things will become fresh. Things you have taken for granted will become surprising. Next, sparks of insight will begin to connect the Gospel story with other things in the Bible. And then you may notice that the Gospel will begin to reach into you. You will recognize yourself and your own life in some of the characters that meet Jesus. Then there will come a moment when it is to *you* that Jesus is speaking, *you* that he touches, *you* that he calls. Your heart will stir. Then it will happen.

I should enter into the Gospel as deeply and closely as I can. The Gospel enters into me, stirring my heart . . . and then it will happen. Is that what it's like to pray the Gospel?

> You are an enclosed garden, my sister, my bride. . . . .
> You are a park that puts forth pomegranates,
> with all choice fruits. . . .
> Let my lover come to his garden
> and eat its choice fruits.

> I have come to my garden, my sister, my bride;
> I gather my myrrh and my spices,
> I eat my honey and my sweetmeats,
> I drink my wine and my milk.
> Eat, friends; drink! Drink freely of love!
> (Songs of Songs 4:12, 13, 16; 5:1)

3. Don't be fooled, now, into thinking it is such a quick and simple thing to become crucified with Christ, even if you are caught up by the fervor of praying the Gospels. That fervor is like a honeymoon. Real love stirs then, but it has to grow. That fervor is just the planting of the seed. Seasons have to pass before it bears fruit, even some harsh seasons:

> Set me as a seal on your heart,
> as a seal on your arm;
> For stern as death is love,
> relentless as the nether world is devotion;
> its flames are a blazing fire.
> Deep waters cannot quench love,
> nor floods sweep it away.
> (Songs of Songs 8:6–7)

I think I understand, Brother Bonaventure. Love grows. My praying of the Gospels has to grow. My quest for the cross must grow.

The cross itself grew! And grows, and branches out, and bears fruit. And Jesus grew to become the Crucified, and thereby to become the heavenly Lamb. That is one reason why the cross is described as the Tree of Life, like the tree that stands at the beginning and at the end of the Bible:

> Out of the ground the LORD God made various trees grow that were delightful to look at and good for food, with the tree of life in the middle of the garden. . . .
> A river rises in Eden to water the garden; beyond there it divides and becomes four branches. (Gen. 2:9–10)

> Then the angel showed me the river of life-giving water, sparkling like crystal, flowing from the throne of God and of the Lamb down the middle of [the street of the holy city]. On either side of the river grew the tree of life that produces fruit twelve times a year, once each month; the leaves of the trees serve as medicine for the nations. (Rev. 22:1–2)

The Tree of Life! You will help me to grow into praying the Gospel, then, Brother Bonaventure?

Here is what I will do to help you. I have several favorite New Testament stories that will guide you to grow with Christ from his origin and birth, through his suffering and death, and even to his resurrection and glorification. I will arrange them in the form of a tree like the one described in the Book of Revelation, with twelve branches that each have leaves, flower and fruit. For each of these passages I will guide you into the Gospel story, and then I will suggest to you how the story may touch you with kindness and healing, how it may inwardly call you to growth and to true discipleship. Through all this perhaps it will happen, and you might experience within you what it means to be crucified with Christ.

4. The symbolic image of the Tree will help you to keep in mind the many dimensions of the cross and the many dimensions of your quest for Christ. That's another thing you may have forgotten: the symbolic meanings of the things in the world around you. Those meanings are still there, but for you they are often asleep in the unconscious. You will need to awaken them, or else your praying of the Gospel will be thin and flat.

How can I awaken the meaning of the Tree?

Close your eyes and picture in your mind a tree rooted in the earth right at the point where a clear spring flows forth. The roots are a realm that is hidden from you, but you know they penetrate deep into the dark earth, bringing into the tree the earth's water and nutrients— nutrients which themselves come from the dead leaves of the tree. Above, the branches reach toward the sky and draw energy from the sun and air. The firm trunk holds together root and branch, earth and sky. Like Jacob's ladder, the tree is a stairway uniting heaven and earth, with angels ascending and descending, filled with blessing and promise (see Gen. 28:12–15).

I can see it. Even the image makes me feel relaxed and at peace.

Realize now that the tree is alive. Its life marks the cycle of the seasons—budding in the spring, sending forth its leaves and blossoms, slowly engendering seed and fruit, and then appearing to die and shedding its leaves to nourish the earth. But then from the dead branches new life springs again, and again, and again. Is it any wonder that the cross, where death springs forth into new life, is called the Tree of Life?

It's not just a pious fantasy!

As the life of the tree circles with the seasons, note that it remains the same in the midst of change. It becomes the unity of the circling seasons as the stars rotate over the firm center of its deeply rooted trunk and branches. The Tree of Life that our minds picture has twelve fruits, marking the full circle of the months.

Dizzying!

You will get used to it as you grow. The living tree grows, too. It constantly reaches higher, and its embrace is constantly wider. Its life is not just an endlessly repeated cycle of springs and falls. Rather, like a spiral staircase, the tree's life circles ever higher, ever closer to the center, its view reaching ever farther outward. The tree symbolizes constancy, but it also symbolizes growth and progress and ascent.

The Tree is so rich in meaning!

There is more. The tree has one trunk but a multitude of branches, leaves, blossoms and fruit. So unity is brought to a bewildering variety of things, placing each in order and each in proper relation to all others. Don't you speak of a "family tree"? And your modern science of biology likes to present all living creatures in the pattern of a tree—an interesting form of the "tree of life." Because it brings unity to the many, the Tree of Life can symbolize the order and harmony of the entire cosmos.

This is too much for me to grasp!

The meaning of the Tree of Life can be summed up easily. The Tree we picture unites heaven and earth. It unites life and death. It unites time as the center of time's changing circles. It unites constancy and progress. And it unites the multitude and variety of creation.

That helps me to understand.

Don't relax yet. There is also a twoness about the Tree we picture. Notice that this Tree grows at the center of the garden of Eden, right next to the Tree of the Knowledge of Good and Evil. This twoness speaks of choice—choice that directs destiny forever. But now notice that this Tree grows on either side of the river that flows down the middle of the street of the holy city, the New Jerusalem. This twoness speaks of balance—the coinciding of opposites that is the mark of the presence and the work of God.

Twoness of conflict; twoness of complementarity.

Yes. And don't forget that our Tree grows right at the point where a clear spring flows forth, a spring that forms the four rivers of Paradise that spread out to water the entire earth, a spring that forms the river flowing through the New Jerusalem. This Tree is the fountain-source of life-giving waters. Forth from it flows the Spirit, "flowing from the throne of God and of the Lamb" (Rev. 22:1).

I think that I am *beginning* to sense the meaning of the Tree. What am I to do next?

Let that Tree grow and dwell in your imagination. Then as we proceed along our path, let its image open to you the different dimensions of each step that we take.

Our path?

Yes, let me sketch out for you the path we will take as we grow with the Tree of Life. We will begin with the lower branches by getting to know Jesus in his extraordinary origin and power, yet in his ordinary life among human beings. As you enter these first stories, you should come to a fresh appreciation of Jesus in his human kindness and generosity. The fruit of these branches may amuse you by Jesus' plainness, touch you with a gentle peace, draw you to come closer, call you to open your own heart. But then we have to climb to the middle branches and follow Jesus through his struggle and his suffering. As you enter these next stories, you should be struck by Jesus' firmness as well as by his patience, and you should share the confusion and the fear of his disciples—and finally their desolate shattering emptiness as Jesus is crucified. As you experience the fruit of these branches, you may find any complacency in your heart challenged, any illusions in your faith shattered, any self-protecting expectations exploded. But then into this bitterness will come the Good News of the Resurrection, and we will rise to the lofty branches with the astonishing stories of Jesus' ascent to the Father, his return as Judge on the last day, and his everlasting reign beyond history. As you enter these last stories, be astonished with the disciples and share their wonder. Be caught up with them incredibly beyond their most ambitious expectations, and with them recognize the power of God at work in them despite their comic inadequacies. As you experience the fruit of these branches, you may pass beyond the dead shell of your preconceptions and expectations, you may let go of any worries about yourself, and you may discover that in actual fact, "insofar as I now live in the flesh, I live by faith in the Son of God who has loved me and given himself up for me" (Gal. 2:20).

5. This Tree has healing leaves, fragrant blooms and nourishing fruit. But I have to warn you again before we begin our climb. You must taste and touch, not merely gaze from a distance. You must try to hear the Good News simply and from the heart. If you imprison yourself in the observation platform of your scientific history and linguistic criticism and theological subtlety, you'll miss it. You'll be like Adam who seized the fruit of the Tree of Knowledge instead of accepting the gift of the Tree of Life. You don't want to make that mistake all over again, do you?

Very well, Brother Bonaventure, I will set all that aside and seek to pray the Gospel. But something worries me. Some people have heeded too well the warning that you have just given. In the centuries after you, people slipped into a mushy sentimentality as they read the Gospel—as if adolescent romance were all there is to love. People got wrapped up in their own feelings, and they failed to recognize their responsibilities to the world around them. If we make that mistake we'll be like Esau, who abandoned his birthright for a cheap stew that satisfied only his own momentary appetite. You don't want to risk making that mistake all over again, do you?

Well, we have a challenge to keep our balance! How fitting for people who set out to climb a tree. But now that we have our methods prepared, our program sketched, and our risks flagged with warnings—in all our planning haven't we forgotten something?

Well . . . I'm afraid of heights! I'm not sure I can do this!

Who *is* sure? Have no fear. Such a thing as this does not happen from planning or from effort. It comes as a gift. It simply happens.

A gift of the Spirit?

6. Yes. We must never forget that. Pray, then:

> Teach me, O Lord, your way
>   that I may walk in your truth;
>   direct my heart that it may fear your name.
> I will give thanks to you, O Lord my God,
>   with all my heart,
>   and I will glorify your name forever.
> (Ps. 86:11–12)

> Your ways, O LORD, make known to me;
>   teach me your paths,
> Guide me in your truth and teach me,
>   for you are God my savior,
>   and for you I wait all the day.
> (Ps. 25:4–5)

Part I

The Closest Branches: Jesus' Origin and Life

Hidden Brilliance in Jesus' Beginnings

SON OF GOD

The Creed

1. The closest branch of the Tree of Life is green with Jesus' origin and birth. Reach now toward its fruit, so that you may savor it. You can begin with the opening words of the shortest and simplest of the Gospels, the Gospel according to Mark.

"The beginning of the gospel of Jesus Christ, the Son of God. As it is written in . . ."

Stop!

Stop?

You have already read more than enough.

I didn't even get started! Where's the story we're supposed to imagine ourselves into?

Perhaps the story is in your reading those words without even blinking or pausing for thought. Have you grown so accustomed to calling Jesus "the Son of God" that you can pass over those words without astonishment?

Well, it is a pretty standard way of speaking. I mean, the Creed that we recite every Sunday is pretty basic, and it says "We believe in one God . . . we believe in one Lord, Jesus Christ, the only Son of God."

But don't you *pray* the Creed? Don't you realize in yourself what it is saying?

It's just a list of the doctrines we believe!

Believe?

"Accept as true"—well, for all practical purposes.

Is that all? Enter more deeply into the Creed. With sharp insight like the eagle's penetrate its words, and in simplicity like the dove's open yourself to let its words penetrate you.

"Believe" . . . You pray it in Latin, of course, Brother Bonaventure. "*Credo in unum Deum.*" I can remember the Latin, a little.

Cre-do . . . Do means "I give." That's odd. *Cre?* Is that *Cor?* That means "heart"! "I give my heart"? What does that have to do with "believe"? Wait a minute. My English word "believe" comes from the same root as the German *belieben*—to choose. At the heart of that word is *Liebe*—love. Oh!¹

Yes, oh. Apparently the centuries have lost sight of something?

"I believe" really means "I give my heart"! I thought "believe" was only a kind of mental thing, an intellectual assenting to something. Truth, something to think about. So the heart has to be at the center of faith. Love has to be at the center of truth. Prayer has to be at the center of thinking.

Yes, and that means you cannot even begin to understand unless first you give your heart.

But it seemed so clear, so basic! "I believe in one God" meant "I accept as true that God exists," and that Jesus is God's Son, and so on.

That is only the thin surface. Penetrate deeper.

"I believe in one God." *Credo in unum Deum.* Uh, oh!

You noticed the tricky Latin syntax?

Yes, Brother Bonaventure. You used the same trick in the title of *The Soul's Journey: Itinerarium Mentis in Deum. In* with the accusative case describes *motion into.* So *The Soul's Journey* is not just up toward God but actually *into* God.

And your "I believe"? Do you see now that your "I believe in one God" really means "I give my heart into God"? And into Jesus Christ! And into the Holy Spirit!

. . . and into Church.

You say that this is just a list of doctrines? Don't you recognize that in praying the Creed you give yourself over into the mystery of God, that you are caught up into the mystery of Trinity, that you actually become the mystery of Church? No wonder you couldn't reach even this closest branch! If you are to seek Christ through the Tree of Life, you must begin by giving your heart!

I . . . *believe!* Help my unbelief!

Open your heart, then, and let the words "Son of God" enter and play within you.

God. Start there with . . . I almost said "with something simple." I should know better! I realize that "No one has ever seen God" (John 1:18). God "dwells in unapproachable light," that "no human being has seen or can see" (1 Tim. 6:16). Everything that we can know or conceive of, God is beyond. Even our images of God are puzzling and blinding: light so brilliant it is like blinding darkness; fullness creating all the universe, yet as simple as utter emptiness. I can't understand!

Of course not! If you do understand, it's not God! And forth from this incomprehensible dark brilliance emerges the Son—God from God, Light from Light. "He was in the beginning with God" (John 1:2). The Word is Wisdom.

That's interesting, Brother Bonaventure. If only you knew Greek in your day! The masculine *Logos* is one with the feminine *Sophia.*

Of course! For the Word is the same as Lady Wisdom, there in the beginning with the creative power of God:

> The LORD begot me, the firstborn of his ways,
> the forerunner of his prodigies of long ago;
> From of old I was poured forth,
> at the first, before the earth. . . .
> Then was I beside him as his craftsman,
> and I was his delight day by day,
> Playing before himt. . . .
> (Prov. 8:22–23, 30)

Son of God! And so far I am just touching the edges of this phrase! I slipped right over it as I read the opening words of Mark's Gospel. Hey, Brother Bonaventure! I thought you said these closest branches of the Tree of Life would be easy! THIS IS NOT EASY! My head is spinning in dark circles of light that are bigger than galaxies! It hurts!

Did I say it was easy? The mystery of God is close, and it is very simple. No, you're right: it is not easy. It is so simple that it is beyond comprehension. But notice what has happened within you.

Well, for one thing, that old familiar phrase "Son of God" has sure become fresh!

It is important that your recognition stay fresh as we go further and touch some of the more earthy stories of the Gospel. Otherwise you would forget to be astonished, and then you would miss the whole point.

Go further? But I am already dumbfounded by things I had taken completely for granted! I have just barely touched the nearest leaf of the lowest branch of the tree you have drawn, Brother, and . . . I am overwhelmed! I don't think I can measure up to this!

Of course not! What do you expect? You are to grow into the measure of the Tree, not the other way around.

This is frightening.

So is falling in love.

But how can I . . . ?

Pray.

O Wisdom
who has come forth from the mouth of the Most High,
touching all from one end all the way to the other,
strongly, sweetly ordering everything,
come to teach us the way.
(Advent Vespers)[2]

JESUS PREFIGURED

The Old Testament
Exodus 12
Psalm 89
Isaiah 42, 49, 52–53
Daniel 7

2. Now that the heavenly origin of Jesus is fresh in your mind, we can return to earth without so great a risk of forgetfulness. And we can reach farther along this closest branch.

I'm ready.

Good. Oh, there is another thing you must be mindful of. The Good News came to particular ordinary people in a particular time as messy as any other. It was a time that is connected with the whole course of human history. And it was a time that the course of history had been leading toward for thousands of years. If you are to enter into the Gospel stories, you also need to sense how the people in Jesus' own time felt their history. Remember that they didn't yet know about Jesus! You need to share in their feelings of expectation and of confusion if you are to enter imaginatively into the Gospel stories.

How can I do that?

Become familiar with the Old Testament story.

Oh, I know about the Old Testament! It tells of a people who endured slavery, wandering, insecurity, war, corruption, destruction, exile and ultimately disappointment. But they held on through it all to a puzzling promise of God, and never lost hope in spite of everything.

That's good, but you must look closer. Use your imagination. What must it have been like for the Hebrew people in Egypt on that night of the first Passover? Their lives as slaves were hard but predictable—until this Moses came along making trouble. Fearful and resentful, they then prepared to flee. The pure lamb was slaughtered, and its blood sheltered their dwellings from the power of death that swept through the land. Then they set out fearfully into the dark of night without any idea where they were going, beyond some vague promise.

That's frightening! But they did have faith . . .

They had to grow into their faith. And the promise grew with them. What a promise was made to the great King David—

> "I have sworn to David my servant:
> Forever will I confirm your posterity
>   and establish your throne for all generations."
> (Ps. 89:4–5)

David was the anointed of God: Messiah. David's posterity was supposed to embody Israel's destiny and God's unfailing promise. But it didn't quite work out that way. David's rule was over nearly five hundred years before this psalm was written. In the meantime there was corruption and war and defeat. Finally the Babylonians came. That was the end: They broke down the walls of David's city Jerusalem, and burned everything. The survivors were brought to Babylon in slavery, just as if they had returned to Egypt.

What disillusion! No more sons of David. There was no "posterity forever" anymore. They must have wondered where God was, for heaven's sake! Some promise! If this is God's favor, what's he got saved for wrath? How long, O Lord? Will you hide yourself forever?

Good, you're getting the sense of this people's story. Time passed. Then it was forty years since Jerusalem had been destroyed by the Babylonians. If God is there and if God cares, there must be some purpose to his people's suffering. True, they understood suffering as the consequence of their infidelity. But so much suffering, and the suffering of the innocent? Some began to see that through suffering the people had become God's chosen Servant, and somehow their suffering could redeem the whole world.

I can imagine how they felt! Who is this servant, anyway? Some servant, if he's meek and suffers! What good is that? Send us a battle-wise king, and then maybe we'll dream a little.

Battle-wise kings didn't change things much. When the Persians conquered the Babylonian empire, God's people returned to the promised land and rebuilt Jerusalem—on a disappointing scale. Three hundred years passed and Alexander the Great brought the Greek empire across the lands east of the Mediterranean. Some years after his death, the maniac emperor Antiochus forcibly set a statue of a Greek god, right there in the Jerusalem Temple. Abomination of desolation! How can God let this stand? This world is perverted, and the powers of this world are demonic beasts who prowl arrogantly about seeking to devour God's few surviving faithful ones. There is no hope!—unless God himself enters the battle with all the might of heaven. Only then will God's Kingdom be secure, and only then will the faithful ones be avenged. In the night visions, hope arose for a warrior king coming on the clouds of heaven to establish once and for all the reign of God by destroying the earth and all its demons.

The "Son of Man" of the Gospels!

Yes. And out of that hope came a successful revolution. The temple was purified and rededicated, and for nearly a hundred years the people of Judah were a small independent nation.

Until the Romans came.

Yes. It was not yet time for the Kingdom of God.

Not quite.

JESUS SENT FORTH FROM HEAVEN

Matthew 1:18–24
Luke 1:26–56

3. Finally came the time. It was not a particularly special time. Rome was in control of the world around the Mediterranean Sea. The Jewish lands were administered by puppet kings who lived extravagantly and did what the Romans told them. Squads of Roman soldiers were stationed here and there to keep order, and the Romans used some greedy collaborators to collect taxes. Jews were allowed some freedom of worship, and an influential class of priests and scribes had developed in Jerusalem. Economic conditions were harsh but bearable.

What a *depressing* time!

Not for ordinary people. For instance, isolated in the hill country some fifteen miles west of the Sea of Galilee, near the great Plain of Esdraelon, the town of Nazareth rested out of the way of most fashions and troubles of the day. The daily struggle to subsist was enough for people there, interrupted by the welcome Sabbath rest and kept mildly simmering by the hope that somehow the promises of God would be fulfilled. Children grew, married, hoped, bore children, aged, shrugged and died. Life went on.

Nazareth!

You remember! Good. Now remember that among those people was an ordinary girl in her midteens named Mary. Arrangements were already made for her to be part of the cycle of births, marriages and deaths—and for a young man named Joseph as well. But somehow Mary realized within herself that this cycle was not the way of the promise for her. What that way *was*, she could not yet see. Since she was powerless to break free from what destiny arranged, she wondered whether she could bring Joseph to understand. That worry occupied her daily consciousness, combined with concern for her tasks and with a constant deep longing that was the base of her prayer.

I remember the story, Brother Bonaventure:

> In the sixth month, the angel Gabriel was sent from God to a town of Galilee called Nazareth, to a virgin betrothed to a man named Joseph, of the house of David, and the virgin's name was Mary. And coming to her, he said, "Hail, favored one! The Lord is with you." (Luke 1:26–28)

Remember how *ordinary* Mary's life is. But at the same time you must realize that this ordinary sixth month of Elizabeth's pregnancy coincided with the sixth age, the moment when the re-creation of humankind began. All previous ages had led up to this point, and on Mary's response to this greeting hinged the whole of history.

But for Mary it must have been a shocking interruption into her simple routine of life. Mary is human! She was a simple, small-town girl. She would have been confused and frightened by the angel!

But at the same time she was wholly caught up in the purifying fire of God, and sheltered by the cool power of the Spirit. She said, simply, "Yes, may it be done to me." And the angel was gone.

Imagine her reaction! Breathless, she could see that everything around her was the same. Had it been a dream? She must keep it a secret—people would think she was insane! Brother Bonaventure, what a fix she was in! Soon she had to realize that she could not keep it a secret much longer. Who on earth could she talk to about something like *this*? What would she tell Joseph? Oh, Mary! This could mean . . . she could become a hopeless outcast! She must have been terrified!

But the sheltering fire had been real! And she could still feel its silent strength within her body. The constant deep longing within her was blossoming into joy that balanced her confusion at what was happening in her life. "The child to be born will be called holy, the Son of God." What her thoughts must have been! "How can this be? What have I done? What will happen to me? Who on earth could ever understand?"

Mary was a young woman most favored, most troubled.

But her cousin needed her help. The woman everyone had thought was sterile was nearly due to give birth, and she would need help with the new baby and with the household. Mary hiked deep into the hill country in response to this family need, in spite of her worry over her secret pregnancy.

> When Elizabeth heard Mary's greeting, the infant leaped in her womb, and Elizabeth, filled with the holy Spirit, cried out in a loud voice and said, "Most blessed are you among women, and blessed is the fruit of your womb." (Luke 1:41–42)

Imagine what those words meant to Mary! "Can this be true? She knows . . . She understands!"

No wonder she sang out! With that greeting and embrace, Mary could release the flood of fear and hope and confusion and wonder and terror and joy that she had held hidden within her. "My soul proclaims the greatness of the Lord; my spirit rejoices in God my savior," (Luke 1:46).

What has happened in your heart as you entered imaginatively into this story? Can you feel wonder with tiny John the Baptist at the power of the Spirit weaving the divine Son into human flesh and spirit within Mary?

Brother Bonaventure, . . . she is so *ordinary* . . . so *vulnerable!*

God exalted her. He ennobled our humanity within her.

She is so sturdy! She didn't know! . . . and yet she said yes. She risked . . . everything! What if Joseph had divorced her? Yet she went on.

Like Abraham, that model of faith, whom God called out of everything familiar "to a land that I will show you" (Gen. 12:1).

Why couldn't God just make everything clear for her?

He doesn't work that way. Ask Abraham and Isaac (Gen. 22). Ask Moses. Ask Jeremiah. God strengthens, but draws forth our own last bit of strength. God guides, but we think we're wandering blindly. God is close within us, but silent. The light of God is like darkness. If you look for tangible assurances, you'll miss God. Besides, if God had shown Mary everything that lay ahead for her . . .

True. She had enough to be terrified of as it was. Let her be.

> For he has looked upon his handmaid's lowliness;
> behold, from now on will all ages call me blessed.
> The Mighty One has done great things for me,
> and holy is his name.
> (Luke 1:48–49)

JESUS BORN OF MARY

Luke 2:1–20

4. Under the reign of Caesar Augustus, there was peace upon the earth.

But what kind of peace? Dear Brother, you are too trusting of tyrants! You are right that it was like the peace after a time of battle. So was the peace endured by the Jews enslaved in Babylon. And the census was probably not peaceable in its intent. An emperor took a census as a basis for taxing and military conscription. It was not a fruit of peace, but a tool of oppression.

And yet it was the providence of God that guided Joseph and Mary to Bethlehem, the humble city of David's birth and childhood. For so the prophecy of Micah was fulfilled:

> But you, Bethlehem-Ephrathah,
> too small to be among the clans of Judah,
> From you shall come forth for me
> one who is to be ruler in Israel;
> Whose origin is of old,
> from ancient times.
> (Mic. 5:1)

Providential as it might have been, dear Brother, what must that imperial decree have seemed like to Joseph and to Mary? Her pregnancy was far advanced. With the cruel indifference of the tyrant, the decree of Augustus didn't care if she would have to travel nearly a hundred miles through hard weather over rough, hilly country in her condition. The soldiers apparently allowed no exceptions. Exceptions are inconvenient. So what if she has a miscarriage? So what if she dies on the way? She's just a poor Hebrew peasant, and we have a job to do. Move out!

Remember though that through her pregnancy, the strength of the Spirit had remained within Mary—but remained silent. Among the things Mary reflected on in her heart must have been the very ordinariness of her life. To the townfolk she was now married to Joseph, and she appreciated his quiet but uncomprehending acceptance of her secret. She could not comprehend it herself! Everything was so . . . normal! Was the angel's visit after all a dream? Routinely she prepared for the birth.

And then this decree came, uprooting them from home and family at the most critical time! Mary knew the risks. Brother Bonaventure, how her faith must have been taxed! If this child is really of God, how could God allow this? How can this really be happening?

She must have known then exactly how Abraham felt when God said, "Take your son Isaac, your only one, whom you love, and . . . offer him up as a holocaust" (Gen. 22:2). With stark, determined faith and with dry-mouthed anguish, she and Joseph set out.

Of course there was no room for them in any human dwelling. No room anywhere near the town! There was no help for them, either. I can imagine it! "Joseph, I'm feeling . . . we must find shelter, the baby is coming!" A rough shelter for animals—at least it will cut the wind. "Hurry!" The straw will soften the ground a little. They were so alone! . . . and afraid. Then the unstoppable roller coaster of labor. Hang on. Leave everything familiar and go into a land I will show you . . .

And yet . . . a beautiful, perfect baby boy was born. Mary took him to her breast. Nothing else mattered, not even their absurdly desperate situation. Mary rested quietly with her baby, lulled by the rhythmic breathing of the animals in the desolate plainness of the dark stable.

The story continues. "Now there were shepherds in that region living in the fields and keeping the night watch over their flock."

Shepherds were so far out on the fringe of society that they lived in the fields. It was not that they were looked down upon as a "low class"; most people hardly knew they existed!

Why shepherds, Brother Bonaventure? You couldn't find any less likely candidates for spreading news.

True! But it was into their silent routine of watching sheep and stars that the angel came. Then the sky was filled with music and praise. And the shepherds found each other in their astonishment and set out for the stable.

I can imagine: They burst into the dim stable, but stopped short at Mary's fearful expression. What are you doing here? Please let us stay just a little longer.

We're here because . . . the angels!

Angels?

They said . . . and it's true! And this is the infant!

Angels!

"And Mary kept all these things, reflecting on them in her heart." It had not been a dream.

Now, then, as you embrace that divine manger and keep watch with the shepherds, what is happening within *your* heart?

I had always thought . . . that everything was so divinely *arranged,* and Mary and Joseph knew exactly what was happening. But . . . they didn't know! They were desperate and afraid and confused. They went through so terribly hard a time!

It *was* divinely arranged.

Not so they would notice!

So how is that different from the way God always operates?

You mean we have our hopes and expectations, and then things happen to us and our plans get wrecked and we get completely confused and lost and frustrated, and things turn out crazy . . .

. . . and angels sing.

It would help if we could hear the angels!

That's for the shepherds—the ones who are touched by what God is doing in your life, but that you don't notice. Maybe you'll find out later.

And in the meantime?

You go on.

And in all this confusion and ambiguity of my life . . .

God is at work: "Glory to God in the highest and on earth peace" . . .

It would help if we could hear the angels.

Come! We have touched only the first branch. Onward!

In my failures too?

Remember, this is a cross we're mounting. Upward! . . .

On earth peace . . .

Humility in Jesus' Conduct

Now that we have tasted the first of the twelve fruits of the Tree of Life, you have touched the paradox of Jesus' extraordinary origin and his entry into ordinary human life. You have also felt in your own heart the joyful confusion that filled the heart of his young mother. Perhaps now you can see the work of God in your own ordinary life, and you can begin to open your heart. Can we pass on now to the second branch? Its leaves are stories of Jesus' childhood, and its fruit is the humility he shows forth in those stories.

I am still dizzy from the first branch, Brother Bonaventure. We started in heavenly eternity and ended in a pitiful animal shelter. We came to know Mary, too—such a strong young woman! Such faith in a God who provided choirs of angels, but not hotel reservations and a midwife. That first branch was like a roller coaster!

You talk like someone newly in love, bouncing between joy and dismay. Step onto this branch of Jesus' family life, which is a little more settled.

JESUS CONFORMED TO HIS FOREFATHERS

Luke 2:21

5. On the eighth day of his life, Jesus was circumcised just like any other ordinary Jewish boy. Mary's son followed the custom of generations before him, from Abraham throughout the Old Testament history. By this ritual the Covenant was reaffirmed once again—the union of God and humankind sworn on Sinai. (Yet this child in himself was the ultimate union of God and humankind.) Jesus submitted completely to his heritage, making no exception of himself. His name, Jesus, means "the Lord saves." In this moment when he submitted helplessly to wounding and shedding of blood, the means of that salvation was foreshadowed.

This is starting to seem unfair, Brother Bonaventure. I mean . . .
well, I can understand why the circumcision. But after everything
that Mary had been through already, can't she be allowed any
happiness without doom hanging over them? Can't they be allowed
just to live in peace without this constant threat of violence?

Live in peace?

Comfortable! Undisturbed! Happy, for heaven's sake!

You would revise the story?

> Why are dust and ashes proud?
> even during life man's body decays;
> A slight illness—the doctor jests,
> a king today—tomorrow he is dead. . . .
> The beginning of pride is man's stubbornness
> in withdrawing his heart from his Maker.
> (Sir. 10:9–10, 12)

All right, so the end of every man is death. So what? What's wrong
with God arranging just a *little* respite?

> Who is this that obscures divine plans with words of ignorance?
> Gird up your loins now, like a man;
> I will question you, and you tell me the answers!
> (Job 38: 2–3)

Uh, oh.

Did you miss the last words spoken then by the teacher of
wisdom, "stubbornness in withdrawing his heart from his Maker"?

That means knuckle under, huh? Ears open, mouth shut?

Hardly! Why, Job was praised precisely because he *did* raise nasty
questions to God (Job 42: 7–8). But he learned . . .

> I know that you can do all things,
> and that no purpose of yours can be hindered.
> I have dealt with great things that I do not understand;
> things too wonderful for me, which I cannot know.
> I had heard of you by word of mouth,
> but now my eye has seen you.
> Therefore I disown what I have said,
> and repent in dust and ashes.
> (Job 42: 1–6)

Let go of expectations. Jesus was one with God, yet he made no
special claims. How should you have any basis for making claims
on God? Let God be God, and follow . . .

> The beginning of wisdom is the fear of the LORD,
> and knowledge of the Holy One is understanding.
> (Prov. 9:10)

Even when it seems unfair and cruel?
Especially then.

> The LORD is in his holy temple;
> silence before him, all the earth!
> (Hab. 2:20)

JESUS SHOWN TO THE MAGI

Matthew 1:1–12

6. The good news of Jesus' birth had been spread by the shepherds among the humble of the land. Soon someone must have given more adequate shelter to the young family. So, you see, they did have some moments of peace. But far away, stargazers wondered at a star of good news that would also bring tragedy. They left behind all that they were doing and followed, risking a venture into a land known for its hostility to foreigners. Meanwhile, for the "important" people, people who felt no need to gaze into the heavens, life continued without a ripple. King Herod continued to maneuver to preserve his power, and the religious powers-that-be continued to bolster their authority. None of them bothered to listen to the news whispered among the humble of the land.

Brother, I imagine the arrival of the Magi sent a shock through Jerusalem! But the Magi quietly left the powers-that-be to their political calculation, and they followed the silent brilliant way of the star.

Now imagine Mary. She sat with her baby as the night deepened. She was used to the unannounced arrival of strangers to greet her baby as the shepherds' word spread among the humble. When *these* three burst into the house—exotic in dress, incomprehensible in language, and travel-weary in appearance—she must have felt alarm. But their symbolic gifts told her that they knew, and that they understood. The angel's words echoed. Gold . . .

> The Lord God will give him the throne of David his father, and he will rule over the house of Jacob forever, and of his kingdom there will be no end. (Luke 1:32–33)

. . . incense . . .

> The power of the Most High will overshadow you.
> Therefore the child to be born will be called holy, the Son of God.
> (Luke 1:35)

. . . myrrh.

Myrrh? Mary would have wondered at that, wouldn't she? Why a perfume that a woman might wear? Or . . . that was wrapped into the shroud of a corpse for burial! She gazed at her child—so perfect, and so very small and vulnerable. What do these men know, she must have thought, and what are they trying to tell me?

As silently as they came the Magi left, well advised to bypass the powers-that-be on their return. Just as silently Mary gazed at their gifts, and kept reflecting on all these things in her heart.

No wonder she reflected!

And in your heart?

I am struck that the good news bypassed those who thought they would of course be the first to know, those who thought they were indispensable to God. It came to the most unlikely people!

People who made no claims. God acts in surprising ways! His ways are not limited to what we believe or expect of him. Follow the star, not prescriptions and expectations. Don't worry about protecting your status or guarding your righteousness. Be open to surprises. Then you will step in the footsteps of Christ. Follow, and then you will return home.

Home? By what way?

By the way that I will show you. Remember where we are, and what we are doing.

I remember the myrrh . . .

JESUS SUBMISSIVE TO LAWS

Luke 2:22–38

7. "When the days were completed for their purification according to the law of Moses, they took him up to Jerusalem to present him to the Lord." By law Mary was unfit to approach God in worship, when in reality God had approached her and come to dwell within her. By law Jesus had to be redeemed before God, when in reality he came as redeemer from God. By law Jesus was introduced to God in the temple as to a stranger, when in reality he is God from God, one in being with the Father.

This surely makes law look silly, Brother Bonaventure. In fact, Jesus completely undoes the power of law, doesn't he? Why, in the very passage with which we began this path, Paul says, "I do not nullify the grace of God; for if justification comes through the law, then Christ died for nothing" (Gal. 2:21). And he goes on to say, "For freedom Christ set us free. . . . You are separated from Christ, you who are trying to be justified by law; you have fallen from grace" (Gal. 5:1, 4). Already as an infant, Jesus exposes law as absurd!

Really? Is that why Mary and Jesus submit so exactly to what the law prescribes? Why are you seeing some sort of adolescent emancipation in this story? It says something quite different. Indeed, Paul is saying something quite different.

Wait a minute! Paul constantly fought against those who tried to impose law upon the freedom of Christians. And throughout the gospels only two kinds of people really made Jesus angry: those who exploited the poor, and those who followed laws the most scrupulously. The way of law is *false!*

My, you have a thing about law, haven't you? You are only partly right, and so you are misunderstanding this story. Here Jesus is submitting to the law even though the law has no claim upon him. Yes, he could have ignored the law, even defied it! But he submitted. Why, do you think?

The story tells of Simeon, and of Anna . . .

They lived their whole long lives guided by the law. Are you saying that they are false? That the child Jesus should have denounced them as frauds?

Of course not—but they are different.

How different, and from whom?

They were led by the law to a hope beyond the law, just as the Magi were led by the star's light to a light beyond any star. They were led to open their hearts, and to welcome surprises from God. The chief priests and scribes in the Gospels treated the law as absolute, as if law was all there is. They claimed unquestionable righteousness, and that closed their hearts like tombs. They thought they had God under control! That's why the way of law is false! It's idolatry! It's an absolute perversion of true worship of God and true discipleship!

And the rejection of law, then, is true discipleship? Doesn't it make just as much an idol of freedom? Iconoclasm too is a perversion, you know. Paul saw that. For him neither the law nor the busy rejection of law counts for anything, but only faith working through love (see Gal. 5:6). That is why Jesus submits so freely to the law, just as he will so freely step beyond it later. You need to grow beyond your worry over law. Let yourself go, and enter into what the story is really saying. Follow.

Mary and Joseph went into Jerusalem. That must have been overwhelming for them, who had thought of Bethlehem as a sizeable city. They found their way to the temple, and I imagine them clinging together and glancing about with apprehension as they tried to understand where to bring the two small birds that they had caught for an offering. Suddenly a very old, tall man strode energetically into the temple courtyard, looked quickly about among the people scattered there, focused on Mary's child, and approached. Awed by the brightness in his eyes, Mary yielded the child.

It is enough, Lord, he said. I am satisfied. I hold in my arms the salvation of my people, the light to the nations. There is nothing more that I could desire.

Mary and Joseph must have blinked in amazement at this inspired stranger. She clung to Jesus as the old man returned him to her, and she shuddered at his blessing. This is just my son, my little baby. Yet the angel, and the promise, and the secret . . . What does all this mean? What . . . a sword?

An old woman approached. A stranger to Mary and Joseph, she was well known in the temple, so much of her life was spent there. She came near, burst into praise of God, and then hurried about pointing out the child and his parents to everyone around. Those who waited with longing for God's redemption gazed toward them with fervor. The complacent laughed off the old woman as a senile fool, but gazed toward them with curiosity.

Shy Mary must have felt every eye in this intimidating place fixed upon her and her baby!

Your eyes too.

Yes! Brother, the clash is so sharp between these vast, frightening prophecies and the simple intent of Mary and Joseph just to do their duty! What must Mary be making of all this? She is human: she didn't know what was to come. How old was she by now? Seventeen? How could Mary make sense of this? How could she deal with all this? She must have been bewildered!

Who said she made sense of it or understood it? Yes, she was bewildered, and probably afraid. She had intended merely to do her duty by the law, but the law led her well beyond itself, beyond what she intended or expected. Yet she went on.

Simeon is amusing! Here he is only at the beginning of the story of Jesus, but he is completely content. Shouldn't he have desired to share in the whole story? I mean, we're not about to settle down here on this low branch of the tree and be satisfied, are we?

Let Simeon teach you something. Savor this moment. Yes, there is more to come, but don't let looking forward stifle your living of the present. Yes, there are higher stages of spiritual development, but don't let looking upward thwart your growth in the stage you presently live. What is to come will come at its own pace; don't hurry it. And like Mary you needn't understand what everything means or where everything leads. Take each step of our way in turn, each in its own time. And for each step, touch and be touched, taste, and follow.

Now, Master, you may let your servant go in peace, according to your word.

JESUS A REFUGEE FROM HIS OWN KINGDOM

Matthew 2:13–23
Luke 2:39–52

8. Imagine: Mary woke up with a start. Joseph was shaking her. Get up. We have to leave.

It's the middle of the night!

Now! We have to get away from here—to Egypt.

That's over two hundred miles!

We haven't time! The king . . . our baby is in danger.

Mary grabbed what little they had, and took up the baby.

After a quick farewell to the poor and undemanding people who had given them shelter, they set out into the darkness.

How wrenching that must have been for them! Thanks to the imperial census, they were already exiles from their home town. Now they were torn even from the little comfort of being in their own country and among people who spoke a familiar language.

The trail led through the desert. This earnest but naive young man, this trembling girl and this infant struggled along a way fit for trade caravans and bandits. Some must have helped them, or else they would have died from hunger and thirst. But many insulted them, calling them stupid fools for undertaking such a journey. They went on, and somehow they found a way to live in Egyptian territory, out of reach of Herod. How long would they be exiles, refugees? They had no way of knowing.

Oh, my Brother! . . . how *terrible* they must have felt when word reached them from Bethlehem of what Herod's soldiers did. All those children murdered—the children of the humble people who had made room for them. Children Mary knew . . .

It is one thing to endure hardship and to suffer tragedy. But it is quite another to be somehow responsible for tragedy striking others. So many people shattered—whose only fault was to have shown them kindness.

Such a vicious, grotesque tragedy! What kind of God is this, who permits innocent children to be slaughtered before the eyes of their mothers!

> You would be in the right, O LORD,
> if I should dispute with you;
> even so, I must discuss the case with you.
> Why does the way of the godless prosper,
> why live all the treacherous in contentment? . . .
> How long must the earth mourn,
> the green of the whole countryside wither?
> (Jer. 12:1, 4)

Mary's faith had to lead her through such dark anguish, had to hold steadfastly to a God who did not act as we expect he should. And yet—think what lies ahead!

> If running against men has wearied you,
> how will you race against horses?
> And if in a land of peace you fall headlong,
> what will you do in the thickets of the Jordan?
> (Jer. 12:5)

Are they to have no peace?

Well, from that time years passed without incident. They returned to Nazareth and settled down as an ordinary family. Life went on without surprises, and Jesus grew and behaved as a normal and dutiful son. You might call that peace. And yet Mary's heart did not rest. She reflected on the puzzlement, the surprise, the shock and the anguish of those early days. No matter how calm their life seemed, part of her heart stayed on full alert, realizing that at any moment . . .

Oh, yes! How the alarm must have sounded within her as they returned from Jerusalem when Jesus was twelve.

Where is Jesus?

I thought he was with you.

I thought he was with you!

Oh, no!!

Images of terror drove Mary as they searched frantically through the caravan and then turned desperately back toward Jerusalem. The last place they looked, praying in their desperation, was the temple. The intellectual elite of the city happened to be gathered in an animated conference there in the temple courtyard, avidly disputing with an amazingly adept young man . . .

JESUS!

Ha! How the professorial elders must have gasped as this common woman rushed into their circle and scolded the prodigy that had enthralled them for hours. They were more astonished as the young man yielded meekly to her, and then they were amused as the woman blushed, realizing where she was and what she had just done.

We were so afraid!

You know I must be in my Father's house.

Once more Mary confronted the unfathomable mystery of this ordinary boy who was her son. She did not understand. She kept this too in her heart, reflecting. And they went on for more years of world without event, with Mary realizing that at any moment . . . And what are you realizing in your heart?

If God so treats this beloved woman who so loves him, what must his *wrath* be like?

You will see Jesus being very kind to sinners (except the proud, whom he needs to shake up). But for those closest to him,

> Who will endure the day of his coming?
> And who can stand when he appears?
> For he is like the refiner's fire,
> or like the fuller's lye.
> He will sit refining and purifying [silver],
> and he will purify the sons of Levi,
> Refining them like gold or like silver
> that they may offer due sacrifice to the LORD.
> (Mal. 3:2–3)

Discipleship begins to sound like masochism!

Really? Do you think that Mary reveled in what she had to endure? Do you think God brings sorrow to those he loves because sorrow and pain are good things?

That would be a dark deity indeed.

Have you noticed that this is the one time in all the Gospels that Mary shows any concern for her own feelings? And even here, she is as concerned for Joseph as for herself.

Usually she simply accepts what happens, the kind and the hurtful alike. She *feels* the hurt, obviously, but she does not fight it or let it get her down. Why?

Note that she has let go of every possession, even of the ties of homeland. Note that she has let go of any claim to status that would be violated by insult or slight. Note that she simply follows along the way where she is called, even though it takes her beyond what she understands and well beyond what she can control.

"Yet I live; no longer I . . ."

Yes. There is her discipleship. The sorrow is incidental. Follow.

Loftiness in Jesus' Strength

That second branch has been sobering, Brother Bonaventure. Now I understand that discipleship has little to do with well-laid plans. It means being ready for surprises and for struggle. I have also lowered my expectations in order to savor simple and ordinary things that I touch and that touch me.

This way of love is no fairy tale, is it? "Happily ever after" is an illusion.

Savoring my own feelings is illusory, too—like "falling in love with love." Like Mary I need to greet whatever comes, respond to it, and let go of preconceived preferences and expectations.

And follow. Come, we have further to go.

JESUS, HEAVENLY BAPTIST

Matthew 3:13–17
Mark 1:9–11
Luke 3:21–22

9. The adult Jesus is first presented by the Gospels at his baptism. John's baptism was a ritual that a person went through in order to express repentance from sin and desire for forgiveness. Why would Jesus need to do that?

Matthew tells that he said to John, "It is fitting for us to fulfill all righteousness." So he followed the way shown by the law and even by custom.

I'm confused. What is this story really about? And by the way, Brother Bonaventure, why did you title this story by calling Jesus the baptizer? Jesus is baptized, isn't he? And John is the baptizer.

Enter the story more deeply, and try to answer your first question. Why would Jesus be baptized? Then you will find the answer to your second question.

I picture the Jordan, a rough river at the foot of a rocky desert valley. Crowds of people are milling around at the water near where John is baptizing. Jesus approaches. John recognizes him and hesitates. Then, perhaps with a shrug of incomprehension, John immerses Jesus in the water.

... in the likeness of his death ...

... and then Jesus rises from the water—in the likeness of his resurrection!

And the heavens flash open, the voice of the Father thunders to embrace Jesus as his beloved Son, and the Spirit descends.

So the beginning of Jesus' mission is marked by death, resurrection and the descent of the Spirit, just as its completion will be.

There is more. You still haven't answered your question. Enter into the depth of this story.

> Are you unaware that we who were baptized into Christ Jesus were baptized into his death? We were indeed buried with him through baptism into death, so that, just as Christ was raised from the dead by the glory of the Father, we too might live in newness of life. (Rom. 6:3–4)

Jesus needed to be baptized because baptism needed to be changed by him! People came to baptism in order to express their own repentance and hope for forgiveness. But now baptism will transform the confused heart and will bring new life, even to one entangled in ambiguity. It is God who acts. That is why baptism is called a "sacrament"—it manifests and embodies not only our own attitude, but the act of God within us. God then will act within us to bring about good we may not even know.

And that is why you call Jesus the baptizer in this story.

Something else is happening in this story as well.

The heavens open ...

What do you see?

The voice of the Father affirming the man Jesus as Son; the empowering Spirit balanced between ...

And what happened in your own baptism?

... in the name of the Father, and of the Son, and of the Holy Spirit.

By baptism we are caught up into the mystery of God, sent forth by the Father with the Son, empowered by the Spirit ... for our mission. Come! We have work to do!

JESUS TESTED BY THE ENEMY

Matthew 4:1–11
Mark 1:12–13
Luke 4:1–13

10. Immediately after the baptism and the descent of the Spirit, Jesus went alone into the wilderness. Brother Bonaventure, why does this happen? Why doesn't Jesus simply begin his mission?

The mission of Jesus begins in the desert—alone but for wild animals, without food and with little water, exposed to biting, dusty winds and echoing silence. Now he is apart from the tangle of trivial tasks and trials that tend to crowd ordinary consciousness. And now he is apart from the network of personal support that bolsters every one of us, but that can shield us from harsh truth about ourselves.

But why did he need that? As Son of God, isn't he divinely aware and ready for his mission?

Don't forget that he is fully human, too. And it is part of humanity not to know the future, and not to know fully where God's call leads. Jesus had to sort out his mission, just as you and I must. And then he had to act in uncertainty and hope, just as you and I must. Remember that

> we do not have a high priest who is unable to sympathize with our weaknesses, but one who has similarly been tested in every way, yet without sin. . . . He is able to deal patiently with the ignorant and erring, for he himself is beset by weakness. (Heb. 4:15, 5:2)

Moreover, Jesus shows the path for us to follow. Now it leads into the desert and into battle with temptation. So he warns us to make no claims: "Therefore, whoever thinks he is standing secure should take care not to fall" (1 Cor. 10:12). And he provides hope and courage for us by exposing the temptations and overcoming them.

How can someone with family responsibilities leave everything and flee into the desert? Is Jesus showing a path here that is just for monks and nuns? Are we lay people left behind, confined to the lower branches of the spiritual tree?

Wait. Let me show you how to be led by the Spirit into the desert. And then let me warn you about the kind of temptations Jesus meets.

I'm waiting.

The desert is a place apart from human busyness—unplowed, harnessed to no utilitarian purpose, simple and basic and free upon the earth. Within your own mind and heart there is much busyness, and there is supposed to be. Otherwise how would we live? And yet outside the fences of that busyness, beneath the plowed surface, beyond the reach of purposes and desires, your heart has its own place of hidden silence. At the center of that desert place is the constant deep hunger that reaches beyond any food and any rest short of God. That is the fountain source of prayer. But wild beasts prowl in the desert, too—and perhaps that is why many people shun the hidden silence within and instead flee into busyness, into escapist fantasies, or into false securities. And the most grotesque temptations lurk there, too, masquerading as angels of light.

How do I find this desert place? Should I seek it? Is it safe?

The Spirit drove Jesus into the desert. The Spirit may lead you there as well. One way that leads there is the way of suffering and detachment that we just walked together with Mary. Suffering and disappointment can lead us there if we don't lose our way in bitterness or vengeful anger. Another way that can lead there is a crisis that halts our busyness, like a sickness or the loss of a job. And you may seek the inner desert by reflection, by leaving your routine behind for restful meditation—though you risk being misled in a fog of sweet emotions away from the stark, unflattering wilderness. But once you have found the desert by whatever path the Spirit leads you, you can then return to it, even a moment at a time. A moment's return can puncture your illusions so that you let go of any claims; a moment's return can restore your strength and courage.

But isn't it dangerous? The beasts and the temptations!

Don't be afraid. Remember that you are not alone in this desert. This story shows that Jesus is there before you. The beasts reflect your own dark side. If you let go of any claims and accept your own spiritual ambiguity, then the beasts will be tamed—they will come, sniff and go without harm and without judgment. But the temptations are another matter. These are not the petty struggle with carnal desires that your word "temptation" often suggests. These are *spiritual* temptations, the more dangerous because they masquerade as lofty spiritual attainment.

Spiritual temptations?

Yes, and here you have some special safeguards in your ordinary family life. Living the struggle to maintain a family, and loving real unpredictable people who harbor few illusions about you—that life provides plenty of barbs to burst any delusions. But look more closely at the temptations facing Jesus. These are grotesque temptations that threaten to pervert the very heart of his mission!

"If you are the Son of God, command this stone to become bread." Actually, he does use his power to provide food later on. What's so perverse about this?

By the miracle of the loaves Jesus brought not only food but faith and eternal life to thousands of people. But here he is asked to turn the spiritual power of his mission toward his own material benefit! Next the tempter shows him the whole world—all his for the asking! And he *is* supposed to be proclaiming the Kingdom! He could be assured of success. He could preach a gospel of success. Millions would hear him, would loudly praise him, would send money, and would do whatever he wanted them to! All he need do is worship Satan—worship his success and his security and his certainty and his connections. On the contrary, true worship of God demands letting go of all these things and following into a land we do not know. Then the final temptation is the most subtle and most vicious—to use his spiritual standing to demand a miracle, to presumptuously expect miracles, to try to control God! Don't you recognize the enormity of this perversion?

They point in a direction opposite to the way of the cross. And as spiritual temptations they all amount to making claims for *me*—my benefit, my security and success, my claim on God! The opposite of being crucified with Christ.

A word of caution.

Yes, Brother Bonaventure?

One can make a claim of making no claims . . .

That too is perversion? Who then can be saved?

"For human beings this is impossible, but for God all things are possible" (Matt. 19:26). Courage! Follow.

JESUS, MARVELOUS IN HIS SIGNS

The Miracle Stories of the Gospels

11. There are some common elements in most of the Gospel stories of Jesus' miracles. Someone is hurt or broken, someone with no claim upon Jesus except helpless need. Then Jesus gently heals, or cleanses, or even restores life—and so reveals the power of God at work in him. In response the people are astonished, amazed. They recognize God present in this apparently ordinary man, and they believe.

But there was an odd limit to his strength, wasn't there? "And he did not work many mighty deeds there because of their lack of faith" (Matt. 13:58). Does his power depend on others' faith?

Note that the people in that story claimed to know everything about him, and they were not open to surprises. He stepped beyond their expectations, and so they took offense at him. There were others, too, who demanded a sign of proof from Jesus, as if they had the right to certify him. No miracle for them!

> "An evil and unfaithful generation seeks a sign, but no sign will be given it except the sign of Jonah the prophet. Just as Jonah was in the belly of the whale three days and three nights, so will the Son of Man be in the heart of the earth three days and three nights."
> (Matt. 12:39–40)

Even when he rises from the dead, they will close their hearts to astonishment and instead try to cover up the resurrection in order to maintain their status and authority. Do you see how dangerous the spiritual temptations are? The scribes and the Pharisees fall to every one of them, yet consider themselves saved beyond question.

Such grotesque delusion! But if a person is convinced of his own rightness, how easy to fall into it. How easy to miss the healing power of Jesus.

Let your own heart join the leper, the centurion, and Martha and Mary: recognize your need of healing, and let the astonishing power of Christ strengthen you.

JESUS TRANSFIGURED

Matthew 17: 1–8
Mark 9: 1–13
Luke 9: 28–36

12. In these three Gospels, Jesus brings his disciples by his words and his miracles to recognize who he is: "You are the Messiah, the Son of the living God!" (Matt. 16:16). But they had a hard time learning that lesson, didn't they?

Peter had a very definite idea of what "messiah" meant. In his mind would be the grand prophecies of an everlasting kingdom of David. He would think of the Son of Man coming on the clouds of heaven to receive dominion, glory and kingship. He expected all these things to be fulfilled in Jesus. So did the others: they were asking for power positions in his government when he took over the kingdom from the Romans.

Uh, oh. Then he began to teach them that he must suffer greatly and be rejected and murdered. Hardly what they expected!

That was too much for Peter: he took Jesus aside and began to rebuke him. Jesus stung him: "Get behind me, Satan. You are thinking not as God does, but as human beings do" (Mark 8: 33). What a crushing disillusion! Peter and the others thought they were on a glory road, and now they discover that their road leads to the skull place and a cross! They thought they believed, and now they discover that the expectation of their faith is false. They thought they were good disciples, and now they learn that they understand nothing at all!

Once again God is full of surprises. Brother Bonaventure, why are God's surprises for those near him mostly unpleasant ones?

A pleasant surprise comes almost immediately. Peter, James and John had thought they understood Jesus, they had been shattered in their illusions, and now in their disillusion they were ready for something completely beyond their expectations. Then Jesus took them up a high mountain apart by themselves . . .

Oh, and Jesus was transformed right in front of them!

And with him were Moses and Elijah—the Law and Prophets that testified to the centuries of waiting for Jesus. The thundering voice of God spoke as at Jesus' baptism, making manifest the ever-present power of Trinity that was catching up all humanity in the saving work of Jesus. The brilliance of resurrection . . .

But Peter got all confused, poor klutz, until they all hit the dirt in terror before the voice of God. They were completely overwhelmed! The heavenly strength of Jesus scared the daylights out of them!

Now they were ready to believe without preconceptions or expectations. They knew they had no claim on such power. Now they might be able to face what lay ahead.

Brother Bonaventure, you talk of their serene enjoyment in contemplating the transfigured Jesus. But they were frightened, terrified, spiritually pulverized! You speak of heavenly repose. But they were glued shuddering to the ground like a green soldier during an artillery barrage!

But that was before Jesus touched them with his strength. "Rise, and do not be afraid."

And then?

They returned down the mountain, silent as if nothing had happened. And they went on along the way, without their illusions.

And now, without our illusions and lifted by the strength of Christ—

Yes, you too: rise, and do not be afraid.

4

The Fullness of His Care

On that last branch I recognized that I am reaching beyond myself, beyond what I know I can handle. What have I undertaken? Such risks there are, and such plentiful opportunities for glorious disaster! And these are the *low* branches of the Tree of Life! How can I go on?

Have you missed the point of the branch we just touched?

"The loftiness of Jesus' strength."

Why are you terrified, O you of little faith? Jesus tranforms our weakness. Through the sacraments and through the ordinary events of your life, Jesus touches you and gives you his strength.

Ordinary events of life! That's where I'm *most* worried about disasters!

Let go of the weight of your worry, and you will be free to climb.

Easier said than done!

Who's doing the doing?

. . . Oh. But I'm still shaky! I know Jesus' strength is there for those who acknowledge their weakness and turn to him. But what happens to us who are so confused that we don't *know* that we need to seek Jesus?

Rise, and do not be afraid. Come, follow.

JESUS, CARING SHEPHERD

Luke 15: 4–10
Matthew 18: 12–14

13. The lost sheep in this story probably had no idea that something was wrong. The sheep did not seek the shepherd; the shepherd left everything to search for the sheep, and then rejoiced when he found it.

If I were that shepherd, I would be more inclined to scold the dickens out of the dumb critter!

The good shepherd did not blame the sheep for being dumb and confused.

Thank heavens for that!

> If you, O LORD, mark iniquities,
>   LORD, who can stand?
> But with you is forgiveness,
>   that you may be revered.
> (Ps. 130: 3–4)

Notice that Jesus didn't set up a consulting office and wait for people to come to him; he walked throughout the hot, rough country and did without rest, meals, or any kind of security for the sake of the lost sheep. He went out of the way to show respect to those who were shunned by respectable people, and to bring forgiveness and acceptance to those who were rejected and condemned.

Like the woman caught in adultery.

Picture that story in your heart (John 8:3–11). Here was a young woman driven by who knows what passion and desperation to a love bed outside the law. Whatever solace she sought there was shattered as righteous accusers burst in, ripped her from the bed and dragged her out among the staring public right into the temple courtyard. They shamed her so deeply that she would welcome the death they threatened with their bashing rocks. What agony for her! And these people so secure in their righteousness that they could *kill* and feel justified! How lucky for the woman that they tried to use her to embarrass Jesus. They forced her to stand right in the middle of the hateful crowd in the temple courtyard. She stood quaking, head down and eyes pressed shut, in silent terror waiting, waiting for the impact of death-dealing rocks. But . . . there was only silence. Blinking, she looked up and around the courtyard . . . empty. "Where are they? Has no one condemned you?" There was only Jesus, and from him came forgiveness and new life.

What perfect irony! The righteous ones are embarrassed. The self-serving, vicious hatred behind their zeal for virtue is exposed. And the poor woman who expected only shame and death was accepted and healed! But do I really have to go through such a catastrophic scandal in order to have Jesus' care reach to me?

Oh, no. Look at Zacchaeus (Luke 19: 1–10). Zacchaeus was a tax collector, a collaborator with the Romans. The people of Jericho hated him for his conniving with the enemy and for his wealth. In turn, he made sure that he was the image of dignity and respectability—not too great a challenge for a man of his means. Like the dumb sheep, he hadn't the slightest inkling that he was lost and needed salvation. He was curious about this wonder-working prophet. But he was so short that he couldn't see over the crowd! His frustrated curiosity led him to abandon all his carefully manicured dignity, and he scrambled up a sycamore tree!

Hilarious! He forgot his pretensions for just one ridiculous moment, and that gave Jesus his chance. Jesus looked up and called him—and transformed his life just like that.

Are you still worried over what happens to people who are too confused to recognize their need for Jesus? "The Son of Man has come to seek and to save what was lost."

JESUS MOVED TO TEARS

Luke 19:41–44

14. But some he could not reach, even with the selfless care of the shepherd: those righteous ones so blind that they thought they had no need of repentance, those righteous ones so vicious that they felt justified even in killing, those righteous ones so perverted that they saw Jesus as a threat to their status and authority. "If this day you only knew what makes for peace—but now it is hidden from your eyes." Even toward them he feels not bitterness but sorrow. His sharp words to them are like slaps to waken them to repentance, but they respond with rigid self-protection. There is nothing he can do! And so he weeps over the lost city.

Brother Bonaventure, such self-deception is so easy to slip into, and so hard to detect and avoid! The very ones who sought spiritual perfection were the ones who rejected Jesus. Is it better just to be obviously a sinner?

To sin conspicuously in order to have the correct form of repentance?

Don't you see there another form of the same smugness and self-protection?

Then where is the way?

The way of the cross, that leads one to be crucified with Christ so that there is no more "I." We are on that way. But it is given, not achieved—so that no one can make any claim, and so that any boasting or spiritual pretension is ruled out. Come, follow.

JESUS ACCLAIMED KING OF THE WORLD

Matthew 21: 1–11
Mark 11: 1–11
Luke 19: 29–38
John 12: 12–16

15. Word had spread. A wave of popular enthusiasm swept Jesus toward Jerusalem, acclaiming him the expected Messiah. The time was at hand! All of the expectations and all the hopes bloomed in the hearts of the people as Jesus approached Jerusalem. And so Jesus allowed himself to play the role that the crowd scripted for him: "Fear no more, O daughter Zion; see, your king comes, seated upon an ass's colt." And the crowd responded with cheers of Hosanna.

This story seems incongruous, Brother Bonaventure. The Gospels have been sober about Jesus' chances for success. At this point it looks as if he could have taken over the entire nation if he wished.

And lived happily ever after? Yes, there is a touch of romance in this story, like the couple celebrating a wedding aniversary and reliving for a moment the rosy dreams they had as bride and bridegroom:

> Daughters of Jerusalem, come forth
> and look upon King Solomon
> In the crown with which his mother has crowned him
> on the day of his marriage,
> on the day of the joy of his heart.
> (Song of Songs 3:11)

Just as the couple's love is still real and warm, so is there truth and joy in this triumphal entry of Jesus as king into his own city and temple. And just as the couple's celebration is grounded in sober reality, so Jesus is aware of the irony of this triumph. He can foresee that in a few days these same people will scream for his crucifixion when he turns out to be a messiah quite different from the one they expect. But in his care for those few whose faith survives their expectations, he allows himself joyfully to play this role.

How can one be joyful when marching toward a cross? How can I be joyful when I am so riddled with confusion and ambiguity?

This is a moment of triumph in spite of the irony—perhaps because of it! And the anniversary celebration of joy and love is perhaps even enhanced by that silent awareness of struggle and ambiguity. Must you have everything assured, everything under control?

It would be easier.

It would be impossible! Unless you prefer illusion. "I rejoice . . . in my weakness. So the power of Christ may dwell. . . ."

You mean it doesn't matter. All that matters is . . .

Your king comes! Let go, rejoice! . . . and follow.

JESUS, HOLY BREAD

Matthew 26:17–29
Mark 14:12–25
Luke 22:7–38
John 13–17

16. The full measure of Jesus' care is shown in the last supper. He knew that his hour had come, and having loved his own in the world, he loved them to the end. This was the Passover, remembering that night when the shadow of death passed over the Israelites in Egypt, and then they passed over the sea from slavery into the freedom of the people of God. Jesus shared the Passover lamb with his closest disciples—he who was the Lamb of God that frees the world from sin. Jesus is near the end of his mission. He has come to reveal the Father and so bring people to eternal life. Now he is going to return to the Father through the dark passage ahead. Then the disciples will have to carry on his mission.

But—are they *ready* for such a task?

Come and see. Look, in the middle of the supper Jesus stands up, takes off his tunic, picks up water, bowl and towel, and sets out to wash feet like the lowest of servants. No lowly service should be beneath the disciple of Jesus.

But the disciples are too astonished to say anything! Except Peter, of course, who never lacks for words however silly they are.

Then Jesus reminds them of his mission and theirs. This is their third Passover together, and through all these days and months Jesus has taught them by word and astonishing sign that God the Father, whom no one can see or touch, is here visible and tangible right with them in Jesus. But they completely misunderstood! "Lord, show us the Father, and that will be enough for us." Philip? Haven't you understood anything at all?

With the disciples so befuddled, Jesus hardly needed a betrayer! Oh, Brother Bonaventure, you are a teacher too. Is there anything that jerks out the plug at the base of your heart more painfully than seeing how little your students have understood after all that time and effort? Jesus is heading for the cross. Judas has just left. The future of Jesus' mission depends on these confused, unlikely disciples. They are supposed to reveal Jesus by their love for one another—and Luke shows them bickering about *status* right here at the last supper! What a bunch of losers!

Haven't you understood anything at all?

Uh . . . what have I missed?

What is really happening in this story?

Jesus shares his body as strengthening bread, his blood as fortifying wine. In the fullness of his care, Jesus gives to his disciples his presence with them, his constant strength. The power of the Spirit is at work, too, to teach them everything and remind them of all that Jesus said to them. In spite of all their confusion.

So they will live happily ever after?

Hardly! They have much to suffer. And even after the resurrection and after the Spirit has filled them with strength, Peter still gets confused and impulsive! They still make mistakes and have conflicts and misunderstandings! For centuries!

You are surprised? Yet their mission is carried forward, and the power of God is at work.

In spite of confusion and ambiguity? In spite of betrayers?

Perhaps *because* of all that. How else would it be so obvious that God must be at work? Unless you hunger for God instead of for certainty and security, you will miss his signs and his mission for you. Have you ever heard that God worked in a way that is clear and unambiguous?

It would be easier . . .

Ha! Get up, let us go.

It's dark . . .

Yes, of course it is.

I can't see where we're climbing.

Gethsemane. Then Golgotha. Rise, and do not be afraid.

Part II

*The Painful Branches:
Jesus' Passion and Death*

5

Jesus' Confidence amid Dangers

Are you ready to climb? The next set of branches is higher, and it's starting to get windy.

I don't know. I feel vertigo.

Don't look down. Remember what happened to Peter when he tried to step out onto the water with Jesus (Matt. 14:22–33).

He did fine while he kept his eye on Jesus! But as soon as he remembered the dangers and looked to himself—schloop! Help!

But Jesus reached out and caught him. Such is the fullness of his care. You must forget fear for yourself. Keep your eye on Jesus.

JESUS SOLD BY FRAUD

Matthew 26:14–16, 47–50
Mark 14:10–11, 43–45
Luke 22:3–6, 47–48

17. The first thing we meet on this branch is the perfidy of Judas the traitor—filled with deceit and greed and ingratitude. His wickedness and disloyalty are inexplicable. He is wholly given over to evil. Yet the lesson for us is that Jesus did not close his heart even to such a scoundrel, and so we should harbor no bitterness or anger toward a friend who might turn against us.

Wait a minute, Brother Bonaventure. You are shoving Judas aside as if he were barely human. Do you feel he got what he deserved when his insides were splattered all over the Field of Blood? (Acts 1:17–18). Clearly he angers you, Brother. But he worries me. It's just . . . to me he is not inexplicable. I can see some of Judas in myself.

If that is true, you're right to worry!

Try to enter Judas's story for a moment, and see what I mean. After all, Jesus did choose him as an apostle! And he was trusted with a share in the apostles' ministry. He joined the others as they proclaimed the Kingdom, cured the sick and drove out demons (Matt. 10:8). Jesus even trusted him with what little money they had, probably not because he was greedy, but because he was capable. Judas was so absolutely committed to Jesus' mission to the poor that he became upset over the woman wasting expensive perfume on Jesus (John 12:1–7). Why, he seemed even more single-minded than Jesus!

He must have thought he understood Christ's mission better than Jesus did himself! Think of Peter, who tried to correct Jesus as he predicted his suffering (Mark 8:32–33). Master, messiahs aren't supposed to do that! But poor Peter was stung into seeing that he really did not understand. In his simplicity, he accepted that and followed.

But not Judas. If Jesus did not live up to his expectations of the Messiah, or if Jesus failed to meet his definition of holiness, then Jesus must be a fraud! And so Judas in his righteousness took it upon himself to expose Jesus as the fraud he appeared to be. He thought he was zealously serving God's own holy purpose. See why I'm worried?

It's disturbing!

The scribes and Pharisees were bad enough, blinded as they were by their established doctrine and authority. But Judas was close to Jesus, was touched by Jesus, ate the bread from Jesus' hand—and still so trusted his own blind certainty that he would pass judgment and condemn. The tragic fraud is in Judas's self-deception. He mustn't have even considered that he might be wrong. Whenever we pass judgment, that same fraud threatens. Jesus' warning is so crucial: "Stop judging, that you may not be judged" (Matt. 7:1).

I have been there. Maybe that is why I hastened to push Judas aside.

What? What did you say?

I have judged . . . John of Parma . . . my *friend, Blessed* John of Parma! And he is not the only one. I have been there.

Please, Brother *St.* Bonaventure, I am relying on you!!

On me? Don't you understand yet?

You are a saint, held up to the faithful for admiration and imitation!

You *don't* understand, do you? And you think *you* live in spiritual ambiguity! Come, now—what real darkness have you known? Uncertainty in your career? Worry that you might disappoint your spouse and your family? Dismay that you can't point to yourself as a success? You have hardly sniffed the darkness!

Brother! What are you saying?!

Stop jumping around and lean on the tree, you fool, or you'll shake us both off.

Oh.

That's what I am saying! Turn to Jesus, who greeted even Judas with a kiss, an opportunity, a hope, a grace. What do you think this cross is about, anyway? No one is hopeless unless they give up hope.

Surely you weren't hopeless as you went to meet Jesus as your judge?

You have no idea how astonished . . .

Oh, my God, who then can be saved?

WILL YOU STOP LOOKING FOR SECURITY?

Help me. I'm losing my grip on this tree!

No one looking for guarantees has any business climbing the Tree of Life. Let go!

Let go? I'll fall for sure!

No. You'll fall if you *don't* let go, just as Judas did.

JESUS FLAT ON HIS FACE IN PRAYER

Matthew 26:36–46
Mark 14:32–42
Luke 22:40–46
John 18:1

18. It's so dark, Brother Bonaventure. I'm so dizzy that I feel sick. I'm losing my balance in this wind! Brother, *stop*! I can't handle this!

Didn't you want to seek Christ? Didn't you ask that Christ and his cross become part of you, you part of Christ and his cross? What did you expect?

I thought at least that you would be a reliable guide!

Thank you for being so flattering. But don't follow me. We both are following Jesus. Don't look at me. Focus on Jesus.

After the supper Jesus went to the Mount of Olives to pray. He brought Peter, James and John with him. Good grief, they are falling asleep! They're hopeless!

Look at Jesus.

He's . . . trembling. He's saying . . . he's afraid? Jesus is afraid? What, doesn't he know? He doesn't know! He doesn't know where his way leads! Not even Jesus is certain!

What, you thought he went to the cross with divine serenity? No wonder you were so ready to embrace the cross! You and your romantic delusions. Jesus went into the depth of the darkness.

Oh, he's shaking, violently! What's that, bloodstains? What is going on? What, is he so afraid of death? I thought he was king over death!

Not yet. First the darkness.

We're following Jesus, and even Jesus does not know where he's going? Is nothing reliable, nothing at all?

You're getting the idea. While he clings to God, he is otherwise absolutely and completely alone. His mission has been wrecked. His disciples are either asleep or uncomprehending. He is being betrayed by a close friend. The representatives of God are his most determined enemies. Everything is dissolving into catastrophe. Surely he must be wondering if Judas was right, and he himself is indeed a fraud.

Everything . . . but God! He knows God is with him!

Not for long. That will go, too.

He will feel abandoned even by God? Oh, no! How can he . . . go on?

I don't know. He will . . . into absolute blackness and emptiness. At least from this point, though, events will carry him along like a flash flood. Get up, let us go. Look, the betrayer is at hand.

No, I won't! If even Jesus is terrified and uncertain, what can I rely on? Is there no shelter from this storm? Even God disappears? Get away from me, Brother! I'm going back!

The way of Jesus leads deeper than despair, into that sheer darkness.

Leave me alone! Please, can't this pass? Can't I escape this? Isn't there a safe haven for me somewhere? Help me! I'm losing my grip! I'm being torn away!

WHAT ARE YOU CLINGING TO?

I . . . my ME!

FOR GOD'S SAKE, LET GO OF YOURSELF, or you'll be shattered in this storm like Judas!

I'M AFRAID!

LET GO! Stay close, and follow!

JESUS SURROUNDED BY A MOB

Matthew 26:47–56
Mark 14:43–52
Luke 22:47–53
John 18:2–11

19. The wind is whipping grotesque images through my mind. I can't see the way in this flickering light. What is happening?

Judas has led a mob of soldiers and thugs into the garden. They are ready for a fight. Some of the disciples shout an alarm. Peter, James and John wake up. Jesus is already coming toward the mob. Someone, Peter, it seems—good old Peter!—grabs a sword as if Armageddon was upon them! In the flickering light a flash of steel, astonished anger and blood. In another flicker a healing touch, another kind of astonishment that is the confusion of anger. No heavenly armies come to the rescue. The disciples flee, their apocalyptic dreams shattered. Judas gives his infamous kiss. Jesus is left alone in the hands of this cynical mob.

Things don't fit together! Why did the mob think they needed weapons? Why did Peter think he needed a sword? *Why* no heavenly armies, for heaven's sake? In all the confusion Jesus worries over a cut ear! Then that grotesque kiss! Panic and pandemonium!

Things fit together in a web of lies and misconceptions! The soldiers thought Jesus was leading a revolution to overthrow the Roman government. The guards from the chief priests thought Jesus was claiming to replace God. The guards from the Pharisees thought Jesus was out to undo the Law. The disciples still hoped Jesus was not serious about having to suffer and die. They expected the angelic armies! Peter thought he fought on the side of the angels. The guard he sliced roared for revenge, when suddenly Jesus interrupted him: Excuse me, have you misplaced your ear? Here, let me return it. Everyone's expectations were confounded, and they were stalled as effectively as if Jesus had thrown them all to the ground.

Jesus even had to remind Judas what he was about: "Friend, do what you have come for!" And that turned everything loose. The mob acted out their preconceptions. Their expectations shattered, the disciples scattered in panic and disillusion. Dear Brother, no one allowed Jesus to be who he was!

How alone he was then! He was hated by those who should have understood him. He was abandoned by those who should have been strong enough to follow when they no longer understood.

Among the tortures Jesus endured, this must have been one of the sharpest—that none stayed beyond what they expected and understood, no one, not even one. Now do you also want to leave?

To whom shall I go? In this twisting storm I am lost if I try to go back. Can it be worse to go on? Help me and I will try to follow.

Let go of your expectations. Do you count on a heaven of joyful rest? That is at best a promise. Do you expect that the just will triumph and the evil will be punished? Then look at Jesus refusing to call in heavenly armies to defend the just, and look at him using his divine power only to heal one of the vicious. Do you expect to be personally saved by Jesus? Look at the naive young man running off naked and terrified. Every expectation and every preconception that serves to guard your little self must be whipped away in this dark wind. That is what happened to the disciples, and that is why they have run off to hide and cower. Otherwise you risk marching beside the resolute Judas.

What then is left to me?

Nothing. Let go! Follow!

JESUS BOUND WITH CHAINS

John 18:12

20. At least one or two of the fleeing disciples must have turned once they realized they were not being chased by the mob. Brother, do you think they were *still* expecting Jesus to overthrow their enemies, but *by himself?* Maybe *now* the heavenly armies were coming. Maybe they felt they should slip back, just to make sure they didn't lose their places in the new kingdom.

But their disillusion deepened as they saw Jesus so dramatically under the power of his enemies—bound, manhandled, dragged off like a common criminal. He seemed so completely helpless! And it was on him that they had relied for strength! Now he was led off like a trusting lamb to the slaughter. But the disciples witnessed no hint of vengeance upon the evildoers (see Jer. 12:19–20), not even on that traitor Judas! Everything they had hoped for began to topple, shatter, dissolve.

Judas must have felt vindicated!

No—watch what happened to Judas. If indeed he did act out of misguided religious conviction, he learned soon enough that he'd been used—he was just a pawn in a cynical game that the political and religious powers-that-be were playing to maintain their status and authority. He'd been used, and his own expectations and preconceptions fell into smithereens about his ankles. Maybe for the first time he realized that he might have been wrong—but the deed was done now, irreversible. Now the veil of delusion was drawn away, and he saw his own zeal for what it really was: treachery. For him, too, everything he had counted on and hoped for had come to worse than nothing. There was nothing left for him! In his despair he destroyed himself.

Brother—if Judas too is left with nothing . . . how is that different really from the apostles? How is that different from me? Why is the blackness of his disillusion termed despair, and ours not? Am I not as likely to fall headlong into the same fate?

There is one crucial difference. In his disillusion, Judas still clung to himself. In his remorse, Judas felt compelled to disown his deed so that he could again look upon himself as a paragon of virtue (Matt. 27:3–5). The chief priests and elders dismissed him—that's your problem, you poor sucker. He clung to himself, to his shattered claim of righteousness. With that delusion burst open, he despaired.

In so desperate a storm, where is a safe path for us?

Safe? Who said anything about safe? You must follow deeper, farther out on a limb than despair. Like Judas you find your expectations, preconceptions and spiritual pretensions shattered. Any claims you might make are laughable. So let go of them; don't try to patch them together as Judas did. And you must go more deeply still into the darkness, even beyond the blackness of Judas's despair—and let go of your very self.

I feel as if I'm being whipped and twisted and spun about in a tornado! And you tell me to step farther out on the limb beyond any hope of safety?

Yes, if you are to be nourished by the fruit that this branch bears for you. Keep your eye on Jesus! This branch bears his confidence in dangers beyond hope and despair. Follow!

6

Jesus' Patience amid Insult and Injury

What, another branch to climb? Now? In this hurricane?

We cannot rest yet. Christ is not yet formed in you. You have come up here to be crucified with Christ, haven't you? Follow.

I have been dragged beyond despair, and that is not enough? I have been spun about beyond dizziness, and I don't deserve a rest?

You have hardly begun. On this branch, you follow Jesus through worse than betrayal and arrest. You must learn to suffer injuries within and without, from friend as well as enemy. And yet your battered heart will not be destroyed.

I won't, huh? I wish I were so sure!

Not your "I." The heart in you will not be destroyed, all the more so as you come to that point where there is no more "I." Are you ready?

Who is ever ready for this?

Come.

JESUS DENIED BY HIS FRIEND

Matthew 26:69–75
Mark 14:66–72
Luke 22:54–62
John 18:15–27

21. Of course it would be Peter. Peter is so appealing, Brother Bonaventure—so impetuous, so outspoken, so affectionate, so effusive, so eager to please and so easily dismayed. Peter just had to know what was happening to Jesus. So he slipped in to spy on the proceedings, right into the enemy camp like a secret agent. But somebody spotted him. Fingers pointed, eyes turned: You are one of them! Suddenly he was at risk. "Huh? No, never heard of him." They pressed. In fear for himself, he shouted "Jesus? I don't even know the !@*#@#*! man!" Just then Jesus came easily within

earshot, and he looked at Peter. The cock crowed. For Peter's heart, the bottom fell out.

He had hoped in Jesus, even when things looked so bad. But he had also relied on himself, trusting that his love for Jesus would give him courage to follow him, even to death. Now he had a double shattering. Jesus was condemned, and he himself was a failure, a coward and a betrayer. His self was a shambles, gaudy dead leaves to be blown away in the wind. Peter ran out and wept bitterly.

Like Judas?

No, because that was not the end for Peter. His claims to bravery were smashed. Even his claim to be a loyal disciple was inciner-ated—all gone, blasted, dead. What was left? A heart that followed Jesus anyway. A heart that returned to the other disciples, ex-plained and admitted what a fool he was, but told of Jesus and waited for Jesus. Unlike Judas, he let go of himself. He saw himself for the joke that he was and laughed at himself as he wept for Jesus. For him there was forgiveness and transformation, in spite of everything.

But he didn't know that then, though, did he? He just knew his own emptiness and the helpless situation of his master Jesus. Disillusioned, he simply waited with the others.

How is your own heart faring?

The storm seems still. The dramatic pressures Peter faced do not touch me—deny Jesus or die!

This is the lull before the full violence of the storm, the eye of the hurricane. The pressures are there, but more subtle. In order to get along, act as if you are a stranger to Jesus. In order to be secure, don't do anything that would even attract the attention of the powers-that-be, let alone challenge them. Ears open, mouth shut. I mean it's hard to find a good position in your field of work! Don't question anything. Don't make waves. Be a good church-goer, because that's expected. But if you're confronted, dodge, or, if you must, sell out. Do what's expedient. Cover your tail.

Help me, Brother! The fury of the storm hits suddenly! I'm being torn apart!

Have I hit a sensitive nerve?

What am I to do? If I compromise, I risk denying Jesus like Peter. If I stand firm, I risk being rigidly zealous like Judas. Whatever I do, I betray Jesus!

You expect to come through this untouched by ambiguity and failure and betrayal? Let go.

I'll be blown away like dry old leaves!

So? What will be lost?

JESUS BLINDFOLDED

Matthew 26:57–68
Mark 14:53–65
Luke 22:66–71
John 18:13, 19–24

22. Meanwhile Jesus was led before the solemn council of the high priest. Here were the official teachers and interpreters of God's truth and God's law. If there was anywhere on earth that Jesus should be entitled to a fair hearing and a just judgment, this was the place.

But wasn't it obvious to Jesus that this was all a charade? All the proper procedure was just a cynical veneer over small people in big places determined to get him, just get him, truth and justice be damned.

Even at that they couldn't get their act coordinated. Their coached witnesses kept forgetting their lines. The sham would be obvious to any fair-minded person, but no fair-minded persons were to be found here. Jesus remained silent as they made fools of themselves. Then the direct question: If you are the Messiah, tell us!

Brother Bonaventure, what did he know of himself and of what was to come?

Ask him.

Dare I? Now?

"If I tell you, you will not believe, and if I question, you will not respond" (Luke 22:67).

Brother . . . doesn't Jesus *know* he is God's son?

Whether he knows or not I don't know. But even the man Jesus must live by faith and give his heart over into God—even when God seems to pay no heed, even when God seems completely absent, and even when it is God's own agents who are immersed in evil. Listen—Jesus speaks out of that apocalyptic faith that affirms God in spite of everything and into the face of complete evil: "I am; and 'you will see the Son of Man seated at the right hand of the Power and coming with the clouds of heaven.' " The onlookers laugh— this fool has trapped himself even when their snares misfired. The shout BLASPHEMY! rings in Jesus' ears. Someone punches him hard in the mouth. "Why? Aren't you at least pretending to be fair?" Some pretend to believe his proclamation and turn it into a game by blindfolding him and demanding that he recognize whose spit was splattering on his face, or whose fist it was that bashed him. Over it all sounds the judgment, "He is deserving of death!"

So that is where it is to lead. No angels. No victory. Not even one loyal follower. No justice even in the house of God.

> O my God, I cry out by day, and you answer not;
>> by night, and there is no relief for me. . . .
> All who see me scoff at me;
>> they mock me with parted lips, they wag their heads:
> "He relied on the LORD; let him deliver him,
>> let him rescue him, if he loves him." . . .
> Be not far from me, for I am in distress;
>> be near, for I have no one to help me. . . .
> My throat is dried up like baked clay,
>> my tongue cleaves to my jaws;
>> to the dust of death you have brought me down.
> (Ps. 22:3, 8–9, 12, 16)

That is where it leads: No answer. No help . . . just go on . . .

Jesus . . . You must know what will come, how . . . what you suffer now will save so many . . .

" . . . I have no one to help me . . ."

Brother! I cannot reach him! I cannot touch him!

He will reach you and touch you . . . later. For now, the darkness. What can I do!

Keep silence. There is nothing for you to do. Peter found that out the hard way. Wait, and follow.

JESUS HANDED OVER TO PILATE

Matthew 27:11–26
Mark 15:1–15
Luke 22:66–71
John 18:28–19:16

23. Now the horrendous impiety! Insatiable blood lust! Like wild beasts! Rabid dogs! Deceitful, treacherous, screaming . . . !

Easy, Brother Bonaventure. What makes you so angry?

Look what they have done to Jesus!

They?

They!

Brother, you know better. And we have learned something in the seven centuries between us. You can be so angry at "them" only if you think you are a "detached observer," untouched by this evil somehow and purely faithful to Jesus. Brother, I don't think there are any "observer" seats in this story.

How else can one enter into the story?

Look more closely. Perhaps you should focus on another aspect of this crowd that accuses Jesus. The leaders of this mob are the chief priests, aren't they? They want to destroy Jesus because in the name of God and of good, he challenged their status and authority. They could have accepted that challenge, questioned themselves, and changed their hearts. How different the Gospel story would be then! But how much easier to place the blame for evil on someone else! Then the disquieting questions are silenced, and they can go on as before. With the world purged of the evil, all will be well.

The wind *is* a bit strong on this branch.

Look then at the common people who scream "Away with him! Away with him! Crucify him!" Aren't these the very same people who only days before were welcoming him with shouts of Hosanna?

Vicious, treacherous, fickle mad dogs!

Look more closely, Brother. These were people living in a disappointing world. They shouted Hosanna because they thought Jesus was the great King who came to squash everything that they blamed for their disappointment. Did they ever question themselves, or look to change their expectations? Of course, they would have to let go of themselves for that to happen. If they had, perhaps Jesus could have led them to the Kingdom that is different from what they expected. But no, they raged at him, blaming him for all their disappointment. Destroy him! Then the world will be cleansed and all will be well.

The wind is *very* strong!

Are we getting close? Shall we dress the high priests in red? Or in the white of the Inquisitor? The Cathari threaten: Away with them! Away with them! Burn them! And all will be well. The Spirituals threaten: Away with them! Away with them! Jail them!

Ow!

All is not well? We haven't even left your own century, dear Brother. Come and follow! There is misfortune in our town? That woman is probably a witch. Away with her! Away with her! Drown her! And all will be well. The Jews are different, it must be them. Away with them! Away with them! Drive them out! Burn them! Gas them! That one is yours, isn't it, Brother Bonaventure—and it reaches all the way into my century as well. These are communists! Away with them! Conspire against them, send death squads after them, assassinate them, send secret armies to slaughter them! And all will be well. Those are aggressors! (Besides, their religion and customs are different from ours.) Away with them! Away with them! Bomb them! And all will be well.

Stop!

It doesn't stop, though. As long as we blame our disappointments on "them" and refuse to question ourselves, it goes on. The liberals are socialists! Away with them! Away with them! Discredit them! The conservatives are reactionaries! Away with them! Away with them! Embarrass them! And all will be well . . .

Enough! I see! We cannot say "they" did something, for there really is no "they," there is only "we." Every time we think we are "good" and blame the "evil" on "them" . . .

Those horrible shouts echo again in Pilate's courtyard. And in our righteousness we persist in the delusion that all will be well, while the real evil festers within us.

Sweet Jesus, who will be so hardened as not to groan and cry in spirit when he realizes this? That *we* have screamed for your death . . .

. . . whenever we cling to ourselves and blame others, rather than letting go of ourselves. Jesus, may your suffering purge us within, so that we open ourselves to question, to change, and so to light and life.

Steady me! This wind! I forgot how wrenching the storm can be on these branches!

We have to lean on each other in order to go on, Brother Bonaventure.

How? . . . I have fallen into so vicious a trap as anti-Semitism!

Don't be afraid. There has to be forgiveness . . . even for a saint!

JESUS CONDEMNED TO DEATH

Luke 23:8–25
John 19:1–16

24. Yes, there is forgiveness . . . because of what Jesus suffers now. Yes, we can go on.

Together.

Now Jesus is treated like a political hot potato—tossed by the high priests into the hands of the Roman official, Pilate. Then Pilate tosses him over to the puppet Jewish king, Herod, and Herod tosses him back.

> Though he was harshly treated,
> he submitted and opened not his mouth;

> Like a lamb led to the slaughter
> or a sheep before the shearers,
> he was silent and opened not his mouth.
> Oppressed and condemned, he was taken away,
> and who would have thought any more of his destiny?
> (Isa. 53:7–8)

Pilate acted like a bureaucrat. How do we smooth things over? Do what is expedient, the line of least resistance. What is truth? What is justice? Who cares! The crowd is bloodthirsty, so give them a little blood and that should quiet them.

Jesus' blood. "I have not found this man guilty. Therefore I shall have him flogged and then release him." Such clear logic, Brother!

The soldiers were used to breaking the spirits of those selected for their style of rehabilitation. But Jesus was silent—so their frenzy grew and their violence multiplied. They lost count of the blows, and those whips were designed to slash through to the bone. Good job, men. That should do it—plenty of blood. He'll recover some day, and if not, so what? Bring him out. "Behold the man!"

And the crowd screamed in fury.

Pilate had failed to understand why the crowd had turned so viciously against Jesus in the first place. They expected him to act like the Messiah! It was bad enough he got himself arrested. But now—look at that bloody mess! Obviously he's a fraud! Pilate was surprised at the fury of the crowd. Things are getting ugly—some accusations of treason are flying around. I'd better cover myself. Too bad, whoever you are. Better you than me!

"Then he handed him over to them to be crucified."

Yes, there is forgiveness, even for us . . .

> Upon him was the chastisement that makes us whole,
> by his stripes we were healed.
> We had all gone astray like sheep,
> each following his own way;
> But the LORD laid upon him
> the guilt of us all.
> (Isa. 53:5–6)

And you, my wicked and impious soul, why do you not break down and weep? Why do you not repay him with compassion and gratitude and devotion?

Brother Bonaventure, why are you beating yourself like that?

It is so common to forget Jesus' suffering! People think it's all glory! We must remember to shed tears!

Go easily, Brother—you are shaking the branch.

Oh.

Something you should know—since your time it became a practice to work up tears and sobs of compassion, and then to revel in the emotions themselves instead of releasing the heart to repentance and change. Honestly, Brother, what do you *really* feel?

My throat is dried up like baked clay, and my tongue cleaves to my jaws.

Me too.

Can you go on?

Let's go. Maybe together we can withstand this black storm.

Jesus' Constancy through Tortures

The going is very rough now. What I counted as achievements turn out to be mistakes. Friends are distant, absent. Love itself . . . what is it? Is it there? Is it possible? Nothing is solid, Brother; everything whirls and dissolves like shapes in a storm. By day and by night, there is no relief for me.

Let us go on—I know the way is black and bleak, but it does lead somewhere . . .

Where? Tell me! I need to know!

How can we know? Draw now on the strength that Jesus gave forth when he stood transfigured before the disciples . . .

Seems like a dream, so distant . . .

There is hope. Remember only that—hope beyond any expectations and hope beyond any control, but there is hope.

I can't feel it.

Lean on me.

JESUS DESPISED BY EVERYONE

Matthew 27:27–31
Mark 15:16–20

25. Jesus was condemned to death. Then he became a plaything for the soldiers. They must have heard as Pilate questioned Jesus: "Then you are a king?" "You say I am a king. For this I was born" (John 18:37).

I can imagine. Hey, this guy thinks he's a king! But not a king like you'd expect . . . Of course not! Hey, do you think he looks like a king? Let's make him look like a king! And so came the scarlet tunic and the ratty purple cloak. Hey, we need a crown! Thorns will do. Scepter? Here's a reed truncheon. The darn crown keeps slipping! Well, pound it on tight with the truncheon! Okay, your royal highness, . . .

These soldiers judged by external appearances, first in disbelieving that Jesus was a king, and then in mocking him with a parody of kingship. It never would have occurred to them . . .

> He was spurned and avoided by men,
> a man of suffering, accustomed to infirmity,
> One of those from whom men hide their faces,
> spurned, and we held him in no esteem. . . .
> Because of his affliction,
> he shall see the light in fullness of days. . . .
> Therefore I will give him his portion among the great,
> and he shall divide the spoils with the mighty.
> (Isa. 53:3, 11, 12)

The irony is that these soldiers, by mocking Jesus as a fraudulent king, actually brought about his kingship through his suffering.

Brother Bonaventure, did Jesus understand all that as he was going through this torture? Is that why he endured?

That is not why he endured. There are internal appearances, too, and they can be as misleading as external appearances were to the soldiers. The felt presence of God; the confidence that one is right or true in spite of rejection by others; courage in going against the crowd for the sake of a just cause . . .

These are misleading?

Don't you see the error in them? Let me press them just a bit. The unquestioning conviction that God is on your side; the assertion to yourself that you are divinely right and everyone who disagrees with you is wrong or evil; the claim that by standing firm against opposition from others and refusing to listen, you are one with Jesus in his suffering and constancy—these are the marks of the fanatic, not of the true disciple. Look at the arrogant claims these attitudes imply! Look how closely they resemble the spiritual temptations that Jesus overthrew at the beginning of his mission.

Then . . . what *was* in Jesus' mind and heart while this vicious mockery was happening to him?

I don't know . . . but probably confusion. And anguish, and . . . abandonment—

> I am a man who knows affliction
> from the rod of [God's] anger,
> One whom he has led and forced
> to walk in darkness, not in the light;
> Against me alone he brings back his hand
> again and again all the day.
> He has worn away my flesh and my skin,

he has broken my bones . . .
He has left me to dwell in the dark
like those long dead.
(Lam. 3:1–4, 6)

How long, O LORD? Will you hide yourself forever?
(Ps. 89:47)

In his confusion he must have wondered if he might be wrong. In his anguish he must have let go of any assurance that he was doing exactly what God wanted. In his abandonment he just kept going, through darkness and doubt. He could only hope that somehow all this was leading somewhere, and that somehow God would bring it to some good.

As bad as that, Brother? Then how could he be so patient, so forgiving?

Of the soldiers, he would think—might they be justified in what they do? And even if not, clinging to no claim, how readily Jesus forgave! He never turned persons into an evil "they" to be judged and damned or destroyed. He stood fast . . . with no claims or assurances for himself, and with a genuine empathy for those who opposed and hated him!

Gee . . . pretty different from us . . .

Very different from the pride of the human heart that pursues external appearances and the marks of respectability, while Jesus is marked by infirmity and scorn. And very different from the pride of the human heart that pursues internal appearances of clear confidence and the marks of righteousness (even to judging others!), while Jesus' heart knows dark confusion, self-questioning and abandonment.

Then . . . as we are whirled about here by the dark wind of doubt and disillusion . . . are we right where Jesus was?

We don't know. We can't claim that.

Then . . . what can we lean on?

The same stark hope that somehow God will bring this to some unforeseeable good.

And is this enough to go on?

We'll find out. Let's go.

JESUS NAILED TO THE CROSS

Matthew 27:33–37
Mark 15:22–26
Luke 23:26–34
John 19:17–25

26. "And when they had mocked him, they stripped him of the cloak, dressed him in his own clothes, and led him off to crucify him" (Matt. 27:31).

The Gospels tell it so starkly!

But we can feel it nonetheless. In the dark spinning of pain, some flashes as the cloak is ripped off what was left of his skin. Then knocked off balance by the weight of the wood . . . spinning in eerie silence like that when waters close over one's head—

> Save me, O God,
>   for the waters threaten my life;
> I am sunk in the abysmal swamp
>   where there is no foothold;
> I have reached the watery depths;
>   the flood overwhelms me.
> I am wearied with calling,
>   my throat is parched;
> My eyes have failed
>   with looking for my God.
> (Ps. 69:1–4)

. . . they met a Cyrenian named Simon; this man they pressed into service to carry his cross . . .

> How long, O LORD? I cry for help
> but you do not listen!
> I cry out to you, "Violence!"
> but you do not intervene.
> (Hab. 1:2)

Some still followed him, didn't they, Brother? He wasn't left *completely* alone, was he?

Some who held to no illusions, and made no claims. Women. Mary is among them. Look into her heart:

> Why do you let me see ruin;
> why must I look at misery?
> Destruction and violence are before me;
> there is strife, and clamorous discord.
> (Hab. 1:3)

The angels' promise and the angels' song, the secret and the struggle, the silent fear and the quiet hope . . . all have led to this. Now they tear off Jesus' tunic, and all can see the efficient work of the whips. Mary stands unblinking.

> . . . the law is benumbed,
> and judgment is never rendered:
> Because the wicked circumvent the just;.
> . . . judgment comes forth perverted.
> (Hab. 1:4)

He went on to a place called the Place of the Skull, and there they crucified him.

"Crucified!" They stretched him out like a hide, nailed him hands and feet, and then raised the cross. The cross was effectively designed: with the victim's weight pulling down against his outstretched arms, his breathing would be constricted so he would slowly die of thirst and suffocation.

> The whole head is sick,
> the whole heart faint.
> From the sole of the foot to the head
> there is no sound spot;
> Wound and welt and gaping gash,
> not drained, or bandaged,
> or eased with salve.
> (Isa. 1:5–6)

His clothes—the only things that tied him with earth—were haggled over like market goods. Mocking voices, some echoing the cry of his own heart:

> All who see me scoff at me;
>   they mock me with parted lips . . .
> "He relied on the LORD; let him deliver him,
> let him rescue him, if he loves him."
> (Ps. 22:8–9)

Where is God? Why is God silent?

> Indeed, many dogs surround me,
> a pack of evildoers closes in upon me;
> They have pierced my hands and my feet;
> I can count all my bones.
> They look on and gloat over me;
> they divide my garments among them,
> and for my vesture they cast lots.
> (Ps. 22:17–19)

This is *terrifying!*
Come: that's where we are headed.
You can't be serious.
You forgot what we set out for? "I have been crucified with Christ." Now pray that we may be fixed with him on the cross.
But . . . I thought that meant a controlled sympathy with Jesus, a kind of sweet sorrow like what one feels gazing at those paintings of sad-eyed, bleeding Jesuses and weeping, transfixed Marys, with a caring God gazing down. I didn't know . . .
. . . that it meant having your mind and heart torn apart? That all the props are pulled out, and the anchors adrift? That even God is eclipsed?
I can't do this. I'll be blown away!
Of course you can't do it. Let go.

JESUS IMPLICATED WITH BANDITS

Matthew 27:38–44
Mark 15:27–32
Luke 23:35–43

27. Resounding like echoes in a dark tunnel came the mocking voices. Within was only a voiceless cry—

> Out of the depths I cry to you, O Lord;
> Lord, hear my voice!
> Let your ears be attentive
> to my voice in supplication.
> (Ps. 130:1–2)

Isn't this enough, Brother?
There is more pain and humiliation. Next he was mounted up on display with two bandits, probably revolutionary zealots, maybe murderers. Their party preached a cheap, violent parody of messianic hope. Jesus had carefully avoided being mistaken for a zealot throughout his mission. Now he was treated like one of them.
Did the powers-that-be think he was still a threat to them? Or were they just that jealous and insecure? Isn't it always true that those who hold power by intimidating others are weak and insecure? The shrill mocking shows that the common people, too, needed a scapegoat to bolster themselves. So they *still* heap all their frustration and disappointment and hatred on Jesus. Even the bandits!
Only one. The other acknowledged his own fault and failure,

made no claim and harbored no rage. At the very time when Jesus' heart wondered if he might be wrong, this bandit's heart realized that Jesus might be right. Out of that stark, claimless, dry-mouthed hope came a prayer: "Jesus, remember me. . . ."

Think who this was, Brother! One thing that made Jesus' mission so dangerous was the zealot party. Their guerrilla tactics made the authorities defensive, and their reputation gave the authorities a convenient cover for their persecution of Jesus. Without the zealots, Jesus would never have ended up hanging from this cross. And a zealot has the nerve to ask Jesus to think kindly of him?

Out of the depths of Jesus' misery came the cry—"Forgive." And to the bandit he opened his heart to share that stark hope that God would somehow bring all this to good—a good like the flawless garden in the beginning, fresh from the creator's hand. "Listen, can you hear me? Today you will be with me . . . in Paradise." It is at this point, Jesus' most desperate moment, that he speaks words of forgiveness. He is still without assurance, still in bleak darkness.

This is astonishing! I mean, I could understand if Jesus felt inclined to forgive once he had tasted triumph, but now? Now, when he suffers most harshly from the viciousness of his enemies?

Had Judas himself appeared beside him and said not even "forgive me," but only "remember me, don't abandon me," he would have heard the same words from Jesus.

Even Judas . . . ?

Yes, and even the darkness within your own heart that fills you with regret and fear, even the self-deception and delusion within your own heart. There is hope of forgiveness no matter how vicious or deluded you are. Even if you are too confused to acknowledge your need for forgiveness! That is how constant Jesus' grace is, and how complete his forgiveness. The only ones who fail to hear those words are the ones who cling fast to their own righteousness, harden their hearts and blame others, ultimately Jesus, for all evil. Their mocking shouts drown out his loving words.

What must I do?

Do not shrink from following his footsteps to the cross. Let go, and follow.

I'm afraid! I'll be blown away by this whirling wind if I try to step further onto this branch. I'm losing my balance, and I have nothing to hold me firm!

Where do you expect to find an anchor? In yourself? Have you been with me so long and you still do not understand? It is the constancy of Jesus that holds us firm through this dark storm! Let go, for Christ's sake!

This we have as an anchor of the soul, sure and firm, which reaches into the interior behind the veil, where Jesus has entered on our behalf as forerunner. (Heb. 6:19)

I feel so strange, Brother! I feel a kind of balance, even in spite of the storm and the shaky footing on this branch. I'm a little giddy! Did Peter feel like this on the water?
Don't look to your self, or you'll lose yourself. Focus on Jesus.
Yes, that makes a big difference!
Don't breathe too easily yet. There is worse to come.

JESUS GIVEN GALL TO DRINK

Matthew 27:45–48
Mark 15:33–38
John 19:25–30

28. Noon has passed. It is dark now, from the storm or from the veiling of the sun. Jesus hangs, desolate.

> Come, all you who pass by the way,
> look and see
> Whether there is any suffering like my suffering,
> which has been dealt me
> When the LORD afflicted me
> on the day of his blazing wrath.
> From on high he sent fire
> down into my very frame. . . .
> He left me desolate,
> in pain all the day.
> (Lam. 1:12–13)

Even without the scorching sun, crucifixion does its work, and its victims are reduced to a struggle for breath and . . . "I thirst." There was a vessel of sour wine laced with a painkilling drug. In response to the dry whisper someone soaked a sponge in the vessel and put it to Jesus' lips. He tasted it, and shuddered with revulsion at its bitterness and its illusion.

> I have become a laughingstock for all nations,
> their taunt all the day long;
> He has sated me with bitter food,
> made me drink my fill of wormwood. . . .
> My soul is deprived of peace,
> I have forgotten what happiness is;
> I tell myself my future is lost,

all that I hoped for from the LORD.
(Lam. 3:14–15, 17–18)

So he tasted the full bitterness and disillusion that came from the core of the forbidden fruit which Adam took—a fruit promising sweetness and illusory hope. Now its full rottenness is exposed and disposed of.

Wait, Brother Bonaventure, did you hear that? There is more happening within him than bodily thirst.

> The arrows of the Almighty pierce me,
> and my spirit drinks in their poison;
> the terrors of God are arrayed against me.
> (Job 6:4)

There is a thirst of heart and spirit . . . the parched cry of one abandoned in the most desolate of deserts.

> My God, my God, why have you forsaken me,
> far from my prayer, from the words of my cry?
> (Ps. 22:1)

Jesus is drawn into the vortex of death with . . . God silent? God . . . dead? Brother, how can this be?

I told you there was worse to come. The dark storm so far still had a dim beacon of hope that God is somehow there, a soft glimmer by which we can at least . . . go on. Now even that flickers out for Jesus, and he enters utter darkness. There is absolutely nothing left. And he must now yield to that nothing.

Look there, at the foot of the cross.

Mary. She looks stunned. It is nearly over now—and she stands by steadfastly. "And you yourself a sword will pierce . . ." (Luke 2:35). A sword would have been a gentle mercy! Come over close to her.

Who is that with her?

The "beloved disciple." Right now it looks like John—but the Gospel never names him. Listen, Jesus is speaking—"Woman, behold your son. . . ."

I don't see that disciple any more. Mary is looking up . . . at *us!* "Behold your mother."

Oh, Mary!

A loud cry from the cross. "It is finished." And he let go of his spirit.

I am stunned, Brother—in the timeless instant between the impact and the pain. I thought . . . that Jesus could endure the physical suffering because of the constancy of his spirit. But . . . his spirit was as torn and desolate as his body! I thought my faith in him would be an anchor in doubt and suffering . . .

. . . *your* faith? No, *Jesus* is the anchor, all the more because he passes through this veil of darkness with no assurances or certainties. He held fast to God even when God was silent. And we must follow . . .

We are right here together with Mary!

Yes, and with the apostles and martyrs and all the saints throughout the ages. What, you thought you would mount the cross alone?

I am feeling faint, Brother. What is happening?

Now we cannot even go on. Let go . . . even of the letting go. Now is the whirlwind.

Jesus' Victory in the Conflict of Death

Brother, HELP! The storm is tearing me loose from the tree—there is no footing, and nothing to grab hold of! I'm falling, spinning in the darkness . . .

Yes, you must go through this. Now there is no help that you can know or feel. In this darkness the strongest faith reveals that it is faith, not a fact you have in your hand. The firmest hope reveals that it is a promise, not a thing possessed. Now you know that letting go means losing everything that you can rely on for support and assurance. Everything falls away . . . and now you spin helplessly in the feeling of falling.

What is happening to me?

Your "I" is falling away. Your heart must wait, be shattered, and endure.

JESUS, SUN PALE IN DEATH

Matthew 27:50–54
Mark 15:37–39
Luke 23:44–48
John 19:30

29. As Jesus died under the shadowed sun, the house of God was torn open and God's natural creation split and shattered. The soldiers turned from swaggering mockery to dismay, and one of them was the first to proclaim Jesus as Son of God. Remorse split those who had so righteously blamed Jesus for their disappointments, and they returned home beating their breasts.

It seems to be a bit late for that. Remorse always comes too late.

It is never to late to turn the heart—and that is not the same thing as remorse. The harm done in the death of Jesus will turn to a new direction. For the crucified Jesus is no longer just a victim of hatred and injustice, but the victim of a holocaust, a sacrificial offering to God. The irreparable will become reparation; harm will become salvation.

We know that because of what will follow. Does Mary know that?

She stands silent, oblivious to the confusion around her. She looks only at the hanging body of her son.

> My eyes have grown dim through affliction;
> daily I call upon you, O LORD;
> to you I stretch out my hands.
> Will you work wonders for the dead?
> Will the shades arise to give you thanks? . . .
> But I, O LORD, cry out to you. . . .
> Why, O LORD, do you reject me;
> why hide from me your face?
> I am afflicted in agony from my youth;
> I am dazed with the burden of your dread. . . .
> Companion and neighbor you have taken away from me;
> my only friend is darkness.
> (Psalm 88:10–11, 14–16, 19)

She doesn't know! She cannot see ahead to what God will make of this!

She too is caught in the whirlwind, and everything she has lived for hangs dead before her. Her strong faith is faith, not fact; her firm hope is promise, not a thing possessed. Her path has led into darkness, and with Jesus' death she must let go of . . . everything.

It is as if she has died with him.

She is crucified with Christ. But . . . she does not yet know the rest. For now, she . . . endures.

Where is God? He has spoken by angels or by thunder before. Why is he silent to her now, of all times?

Voices and visions are for the beginning of the path. God's presence now is beyond what we know or feel, beyond what is possible to know or feel. His word is silence now; his brightness is darkness. Otherwise how shall we pass through the veil, beyond into God? But for now, silence and darkness.

What can we do for Mary?

Be silent. Wait with her.

JESUS PIERCED WITH A LANCE

John 19:31–37

30. Now that they have violated justice and the love of God, the religious leaders show their zeal for the propriety of their rituals. They demand that the crosses be cleared lest they sully this solemn sabbath of the Passover. To hasten death, the soldiers smash the legs of the first victim so that he can no longer struggle against his own suffocating weight. Mary watches as the soldiers approach Jesus. Please, he is dead! The lance flashed. Is there no end to hurting him? Is his dying not enough? The soldier thrusts his lance into Jesus' side, and immediately blood and water flow out. Dazed, Mary sways slightly but stands unbroken. But the eyes of the disciple beside her flash just a moment in recognition and astonishment.

John!

Only later will he consciously complete that recognition and proclaim the meaning of what is happening here. Spared the breaking of his legs, Jesus becomes the lamb sacrificed for Passover—"You shall not break any of its bones" (Exod. 12:46)—the lamb whose blood wards off the Destroyer, and whose flesh nourishes God's people for their passage from slavery to freedom. Pierced with a lance, Jesus becomes the sufferer who brings grace for Jerusalem:

> They shall look on him whom they have thrust through, and they shall mourn for him as one mourns for an only son, and they shall grieve over him as one grieves over a firstborn. (Zech. 12:10)

As the water flowed from his side, Jesus fulfills his own words:

> "The water I shall give will become in him a spring of water welling up to eternal life." . . .
> "Let anyone who thirsts come to me and drink. Whoever believes in me, as scripture says, 'Rivers of living water will flow from within him.' " (John 4:14, 7:37–38)

And in the disciple another prophecy stirred below consciousness:

> I saw water flowing out from beneath the threshold of the temple toward the east . . . There was now a river through which I could not wade. . . . Wherever the river flows, every sort of living creature that can multiply shall live, and . . . the sea shall be made fresh. . . . Along both banks of the river, fruit trees of every kind shall grow; their leaves shall not fade, nor their fruit fail. Every month they shall bear fresh fruit, for they shall be watered by the flow from the sanctuary. (Ezek. 47:1, 5, 9, 12)

Brother, isn't this the river of Paradise? the river that flows through the New Jerusalem?—at the Tree of Life!

Yes, the Tree of Life. So it is at this very moment—at the moment when Jesus has been drained of life, the moment when he has left those who love him most desolate—at this very moment the Spirit is poured forth, the Church is conceived as the living body of Jesus with all its life-giving powers that flow from his heart, and the power of God is released that transforms even death.

But not so Mary and the disciple would notice! As far as they know, there is no relief, no place of refuge from grief. How ironic and bitter now the whirling memories of an earlier time, of an earlier stage of love—

> O my dove in the clefts of the rock,
> in the secret recesses of the cliff,
> Let me see you,
> let me hear your voice,
> For your voice is sweet,
> and you are lovely.
> (Song of Songs 2:14)

And yet how true and how much more powerful now! Right there in the pierced body of Jesus upon the cross is refuge. There, in the temple of his body, is sanctuary.

How can we tell Mary this in her desolation? How can we help the disciple to see it through the heavy darkness?

It is they who will reveal it to us—after the darkness. Only then is it real.

JESUS CLOTHED WITH BLOOD

31. In silence Jesus hangs, his desolate nakedness clothed only with the last of his own blood. In silence we wait with Mary and the disciple. Our silence speaks a prayer:

> Out of the depths I cry to you, O LORD. . . .
> If you, O LORD, mark iniquities,
> LORD, who can stand?
> But with you is forgiveness,
> that you may be revered. . . .
> My soul waits for the LORD
> more than sentinels wait for the dawn.
> (Ps. 130:1, 3–4, 6)

But here clothing the body of Jesus is the garment of plenteous redemption, a priestly robe:

> Who is this that comes . . .
> in crimsoned garments . . .
> This one arrayed in majesty,
> marching in the greatness of his strength?
> "It is I, I who announce vindication,
> I who am mighty to save."
> Why is your apparel red,
> and your garments like those of the wine presser?
> "The wine press I have trodden alone,
> and of my people there was no one with me. . . .
> For the day of vengeance was in my heart,
> my year for redeeming was at hand."
> (Isa. 63:1–4)

But for those standing at the foot of the cross, where is the greatness of strength? Where is the saving might? They know only mourning and desolation, the silence of one abandoned by God.

Their mourning is like the mourning of Jacob after seeing the tunic of his beloved son Joseph dipped in the blood of a slaughtered goat. Like the mourning of Jacob, this mourning will be changed. Whatever the betrayal, whatever the failure—

> do not be distressed, and do not reproach yourselves for having sold me here. It was really for the sake of saving lives that God sent me here ahead of you. . . . Even though you meant harm to me, God meant it for good, to achieve his present end, the survival of many people. Therefore have no fear. (Gen. 45:5, 50:20–21)

True, Brother, it was nice that Jacob could rejoice to find his son Joseph alive after all! But he had been fooled by a goat's blood. Mary has no such gentle shield. She has seen the blood itself from lash and thorn and lance—blood like a garment woven so long ago from her own body by the Spirit. Mary *knows* that her Jesus is dead! And still she stands . . . without sliding back into despair, without abandoning hope that . . . somehow, despite the silence and absence, *God* is not really dead . . . nor the secret, nor the promise of the angel.

Stay close to Mary in your spinning darkness. You will call on her steadfastness as your refuge.

Mary . . . ?

Keep still. Silently she waits. Stay with her.

JESUS LAID IN THE TOMB

Matthew 27:57–66
Mark 15:42–47, 16:1–2
Luke 23:50–56, 24:1
John 19:38–42, 20:1

32. The darkness of the storm gives way to the darkness of night. Silently some who secretly believed in Jesus come forward to claim his body, prepare it for burial, and place it in the newly cut tomb of a stranger. Gently they take his body down from the cross. Mary holds her son once again, flashing in memory to the time in her youth when she had cradled him in her arms as an infant, her heart even then sensing and pondering hints of this cruel destiny. Now it was all played out, and there remained . . . nothing.

Where are the apostles?

The apostles are nowhere near. These men fled at the first sign of conflict and are still cowering in their hiding place. They breathe in defeat and breathe out disillusion: "We were hoping that he would be the one to redeem Israel" (Luke 24:21). Well, that bubble has burst. Now they wait in anxious silence, fearing that the ones who arrested Jesus might come for them, or perhaps holding on still to a faint ember of nameless hope.

Then who is with Mary?

The women and a nameless man or two. The women have proved stronger than the apostles. Not tangled in ambitions and expectations, they have simply followed as Jesus went his way to the end. Now they work silently together to prepare him for burial. After the tomb is closed, they go their way dazed and dry-mouthed. He is dead. There is nothing left now but to wait . . . but for what? . . . just wait.

All of them?

Magdalen can't go away. Jesus has so drastically changed her life—just by a little kindness to her when everyone else reviled her, just by simple respect for her when everyone else despised her or vilely used her. Was it she who had been dragged through the depths of shame to the edge of death there in the temple courtyard that terrible day? Now she cannot go away from the Jesus who had given her the first real love she had known. She clings to the rocks of the tomb that holds his dead body.

> Athirst is my soul for God, the living God.
>   When shall I go and behold the face of God?
> My tears are my food day and night,

> as they say to me day after day, "Where is your God?" . . .
> "Why must I go about in mourning,
> with the enemy oppressing me?"
> It crushes my bones that my foes mock me. . . .
> Why are you so downcast, O my soul?
> Why do you sigh within me?
> Hope in God! For I shall again be thanking him.
> (Ps. 42:3–4, 10–12)

Hope . . . she clings there, waiting—stunned by the silence of God, her heart suspended in that stillness beyond despair where hope still lingers without any tangible shape or assurance.

Brother, my heart is spinning in darkness . . . And yet, while there is nowhere to stand and nothing to cling to, still the feeling of falling has softened, the terror of the dark has receded. Now I seem to be . . . it is a little like floating, as if I am borne up somehow in this whirling darkness.

The terror of falling and the fear of darkness yield as the "I" falls away and the heart is broken open, without claims and without defenses. It is a gift of God that your heart may enter into these stories, touch and be touched.

I thought I was *lost* when the whirlwind tore me loose from the branches.

You *were* lost. How else do you expect that you are now being borne upward toward the highest branches?

Is that what is happening? It feels rather like floating in emptiness.

Wait.

Part III

The Lofty Branches: Jesus Glorified

9

The Newness of His Resurrection

I feel a strange lightness of heart, Brother Bonaventure. I have found that all the works of my hands and the toil at which I have taken such pains—all is vanity and a chase after wind. My expectations and ambitions have evaporated like a mirage. It is useless to worry over my own spiritual destiny. I have met my own righteousness and seen it unmasked as hypocrisy, my own claim to spiritual stature and seen it exposed as fraud, my own sense of integrity and seen it whipped away like dead leaves in the wind. I have become like rubbish, the scum of all.

But, unlike the Preacher, you do not say, "Therefore I loathe life" (Eccles. 2:17).

That is what I don't understand! I should feel crushed, but I feel light and strong, as if an immense burden has been lifted from me. I should feel as if I am falling into a pit, but I feel … Brother, I still have no footing and nothing to cling to, but … I feel as if I am flying!

You must shed like a snakeskin the "I" that makes claims and demands security. You must fall as freely as from a cocoon from the "I" that desires status and attainment and righteousness. You must break out of the eggshell of the "I" that seeks its own holiness and perfection. Yes, then it is a little like flying. Good—because the only way to reach the loftiest branches of the Tree of Life is to be borne up to them.

JESUS TRIUMPHANT IN DEATH

33. All is quiet at the tomb before dawn. It has been the hour of victory for the powers-that-be, the time of the power of darkness. The Tempter, who has been prowling about like a roaring lion looking for someone to devour, curls up now in contentment. The world has prevailed, with its predictable probabilities, its winners and losers, its profits and losses, and the eternal return of the same.

But it does not know about surprises.

> Do you not know
> or have you not heard?
> The LORD is the eternal God,
> creator of the ends of the earth. . . .
> He gives strength to the fainting;
> for the weak he makes vigor abound.
> They that hope in the LORD will renew their strength,
> they will soar as with eagles' wings.
> (Isa. 40:28–29, 31)

Into our desolation a voice proclaims: Do not weep. The lion of the tribe of Judah, the root of David, has triumphed! And then I saw a Lamb that seemed to have been slain. And all the powers fell down in homage to him (Rev. 5:5–8):

> "Worthy are you . . .
> for you were slain and with your blood
> you purchased for God
> those from every tribe and tongue, people and nation.
> You made them a kingdom and priests for our God,
> and they will reign on earth."
> (Rev. 5:9–10)

The reality is so absolutely different from the appearances, dear Brother! The actual event is so far beyond what could ever have been expected!

Do you know now why you feel that liberating lightness of heart? Here is what has happened: Even when you were dead in transgressions he brought you to life along with him, obliterating the bond against us, with its claims. He removed it from our midst, nailing it to the cross; despoiling the principalities and powers, he made a public spectacle of them, leading them away in triumph by it (from Col. 2:13–15).

But . . . look there by Jesus' tomb. Mary Magdalen waits, still desolate. The apostles wait in terror; Mary his mother waits in steadfast hope beyond hope. Don't they know any of what is happening?

Not yet. But soon—look in the east . . .

> Anguish has taken wing, dispelled is darkness:
> for there is no gloom where but now there was distress.
> The people who walked in darkness
> have seen a great light;
> Upon those who dwelt in the land of gloom
> a light has shone.
> (Isa. 8:23–9:1)

JESUS RISEN

Matthew 28:1–20
Mark 16:1–18
Luke 24:1–49
John 20:1–31, 21:1–25

34. Soldiers had been stationed to guard the tomb. I imagine they joked loudly about that: Guarding a dead man! This will be relaxing duty! But . . . earthquake and blinding light struck them dumb, and they watched in terror as the rock spun easily away from the mouth of the tomb . . .

"Who will roll back the stone for us from the entrance to the tomb?" It was the eighth day: the last of the old, first of the new. The women emerged at dawn after the sabbath rest to continue their caring vigil with the body of Jesus. But . . . the tomb was open! A young man sat calmly inside where Jesus' body had been laid. What is going on here? "Do not be amazed!" he said to their amazement. " He has been raised; he is not here."

> So shall he startle many nations,
> because of him kings shall stand speechless. . . .
> Who would believe what we have heard?
> (Isa. 52:15, 53:1)

The men were skeptical of the women's news, weren't they? Come now, be serious! But they ran to the tomb anyway, with the impetuous Peter the first to rush in . . . but they did not understand. Who would believe what we have heard?

Look at Mary Magdalene. She was crushed. They had humiliated her hero, slaughtered her Lord, leaving her nothing but a desolate vigil by his body. And now even that they have taken away! A man approached as she wept alone. Sharply she turned on him: Why have you stolen his body! What have you done with him! Please let me be close to him! Then . . . "Mary" . . .

> The desert and the parched land will exult;
> the steppe will rejoice and bloom.
> They will bloom with abundant flowers,
> and rejoice with joyful song. . . .
> They will see the glory of the LORD
> the splendor of our God. . . .
> Say to those whose hearts are frightened:

Be strong, fear not!
Here is your God . . .
he comes to save you.
(Isa. 35:1–2, 4)

Mary, do not cling, even in the astonishment that overwhelms your heart. Do not cling but go—spread the good news. "Those that sow in tears shall reap rejoicing" (Ps. 126:5).

Who would believe it, though!

Two disciples trudged toward Emmaus, leaving Jerusalem and their smothered hope behind them. "We were hoping that he would be the one . . ." The stranger seemed uninformed. Yet as he spoke he turned their expectations upside down, and the dead embers of their hope began to glow. "Stay and eat with us." And (just as at the last supper) while they were at table, he took bread, said the blessing, broke it, and gave it to them . . . In the moment they recognized him he was gone—and their astonishment propelled them at a trot back to Jerusalem to spread the good news.

But the others *still* didn't believe!

They were confused rather than encouraged by the stories they were hearing. So the disciples cowered in their hiding place behind locked doors. Suddenly, there was Jesus! Terror and amazement! "Peace be with you." Calm down. The disciples gradually loosened the grip of their fear and allowed themselves to recognize him in astonished joy.

They had heard, but now that their eyes have *seen* . . .

And what is the state of your heart as you share this event that is so wholly beyond anticipation?

Faith is firmer than fact; hope stronger than a thing possessed. Love finally now is real, borne beyond disappointment and failure and emptiness.

What then shall we say to this? If God is for us, who can be against us? . . . What will separate us from the love of Christ? Will anguish, or distress, or persecution, or famine, or nakedness, or peril, or the sword? . . . No, in all these things we conquer overwhelmingly through him who loved us. (Rom. 8:31, 35, 37)

JESUS' ASTONISHING BEAUTY

35. Now the full destiny of Jesus begins to come clear to me, Brother. Yes, he is like us . . . "All mankind is grass, and all their glory like the flower of the field. The grass withers, the flower wilts . . ." (Isa. 40:6–7). But now the wilted flower reblooms beyond expectation, and humankind is given a whole new pattern of hope!

The disciples too are just beginning to see. In their hiding place, during the immeasurable instant between terror and recognition, they found Jesus' astonishing beauty etched upon their hearts.

> Who is this that comes forth like the dawn,
> as beautiful as the moon, as resplendent as the sun,
> as awe-inspiring as bannered troops?
> (Song of Songs 6:10)

No, fairer than the sun and surpassing every constellation of the stars, outshining light itself—for night supplants the sun (see Wisd. 7:29–30), but even death casts no shadow on the beauty of the risen Jesus.

Did the disciples realize what this meant for *them?* and for *us?*

This beauty, actual in Jesus, now is *promise* for the disciples themselves, and for all who follow Jesus—"Then the righteous will shine like the sun in the kingdom of their Father" (Matt. 13:43). What will it be like? Paul, struck blind by the beauty of the risen Jesus on the road to Damascus, says:

> The brightness of the sun is one kind, the brightness of the moon another, and the brightness of the stars another. . . . So also is the resurrection of the dead. [The body] is sown corruptible; it is raised incorruptible. It is sown dishonorable; it is raised glorious. It is sown weak, it is raised powerful. . . . Just as we have borne the image of the earthly [man], we shall also bear the image of the heavenly one.
> (1 Cor. 15:41–43, 49).

The disciples have this measureless instant to taste the beauty of Jesus and to rest in Jesus' astonishing victory over death. How happy an instant! And how happy we are if we can enter into this story to see Jesus with the disciples, and to feel just a bit of what they felt. In that moment every fear for the "I" dissolves like mist before the sun, and the heart is freed to act, risk, laugh, touch and be touched.

> "Behold, God's dwelling is with the human race. He will dwell with them and they will be his people and God himself will always be with them. He will wipe every tear from their eyes, and there shall be no more death or mourning, wailing or pain, [for] the old order has passed away. . . . Behold, I make all things new." (Rev. 21:3–5)

No wonder I am filled with the feeling of flying!

Be careful, now. We are not yet at the goal. We have not yet completed our ascent of the Tree of Life. There is now a moment of joyful rest, yes—but only a moment.

JESUS PLACED OVER THE WORLD

Matthew 28:16–20
Mark 16: 14–18

36. Jesus drew the disciples out of their nest of fear. In response to his call, they climbed a mountain to meet him again. "All power in heaven and on earth has been given to me."

Oh, and how the disciples had hungered for that day when Jesus would come into his messianic power! That would be the day when they thought their own naive ambitions would be fulfilled, "one at your right and the other at your left, in your kingdom" (Matt. 20:21).

Yes, this was that day. But their hunger was forgotten now, and their ambitions long since abandoned. Everything was different from what they expected, and they themselves were different. As they passed through the darkness of Jesus' suffering and death, their constant unspoken question was, "How long, O Lord? Will you hide yourself forever?" But now—

> With awe-inspiring deeds of justice you answer us,
>   O God our savior,
> The hope of all the ends of the earth
>   and of the distant seas.
> (Ps. 65:6)

And Jesus himself had let go of his own equality with God and emptied himself, becoming like us in confusion and ignorance and struggle. He had humbled himself, following the dark path ahead all the way to death, even death on a cross.

> Because of this, God greatly exalted him
> and bestowed on him the name
> that is above every name,
> that at the name of Jesus
> every knee should bend,
> of those in heaven and on earth and under the earth,
> and every tongue confess that
> Jesus Christ is Lord,
> to the glory of God the Father.
> (Phil. 2:9–11)

Everything is changed! Everything is transformed!

But this is just the beginning. "Go, therefore, and make disciples of all nations." They have work to do. As Jesus comes into his glory, their role will be to glorify him, to tell and retell the story, to call all to faith—and to show the way through darkness in a hope beyond hope. In that way Jesus' power will be manifest over the whole earth.

But how are the disciples to do that? They are still the pitiful crew that broke and ran at the first real sign of trouble. Peter the denyer is still impetuous. And yet they have been changed, too:

> But as for me, I am filled with power,
> with the spirit of the LORD,
> with authority and with might.
> (Mic. 3:8)

What is really different, now that they have come through all that has passed, is that they know—in spite of failure, defeat, disillusion, and even death—"Behold, I am with you always, until the end of the age."

10

The Loftiness of His Ascension

We can see so far from these branches, Brother Bonaventure!

And how is your heart as we are borne up to this height?

My heart? Fine, I suppose. Why do you ask? Brother, look at the earth spread out below us, and look into the heavens opening above us!

Yes, look. Much is happening! And there is much to be done!

JESUS, LEADER OF HIS ARMY

Acts 1:6–11

37. Forty days have passed—a mirror to the Hebrew people's time between slavery and the promised land, and to the time of Jesus' skirmish with the Tempter. Time enough to change, and time enough to be changed.

The disciples still have not understood, have they, Brother? And the old ways of hoping still pop into their minds. "Are you at this time going to restore the kingdom to Israel?"

Jesus brushes that aside: "It is not for you to know. . . . But you will receive power, and you will be my witnesses . . . to the ends of the earth."

Then, I imagine, the disciples' minds filled with questions like "How? What do you mean? Who, us?" And before they could even open their mouths, Jesus was lifted up into the sky, and a cloud hid him from their sight.

The disciples stood astonished, staring dumbly into the sky as Jesus disappeared. "Men of Galilee . . . HEY! Snap out of it!" Startled, they returned to their own reality. "There will be time later to look for Jesus coming again on the clouds of heaven. For now, didn't you hear what he said? Get ready! You have work to do!" So they returned to Jerusalem.

But . . . what was happening to Jesus?

Meanwhile Jesus was completing his own mission. No, the earthly kingdom was not being restored to Israel. But like a new Joshua, Jesus was storming heaven like that leader who had led the invasion of the promised land. The wall of heaven was being breached by the cross:

> God arises; his enemies are scattered,
> and those who hate him flee before him. . . .
> You have ascended on high, taken captives,
> received men as gifts—
> even rebels; the LORD God enters his dwelling.
> Blessed day by day be the Lord,
> who bears our burdens; God, who is our salvation. . . .
> God gives a home to the forsaken;
> he leads forth prisoners to prosperity.
> (Ps. 68:2, 19–20, 7)

For the disciples and for all who follow Jesus, a whole new realm of hope is opened: "Through the blood of Jesus we have confidence of entrance into the sanctuary by the new and living way he opened for us through the veil, that is, his flesh" (Heb. 10:19–20).

Brother, I see that it is no longer a question of "Shall *I* be saved?" On the contrary: "You are no longer strangers and sojourners, but you are fellow citizens with the holy ones and members of the household of God" (Eph. 2:19).

There is more. Jesus brings renewal to heaven itself as he ascends, reversing the defection of the fallen angels. So the heavenly city rejoices, because the redeemed people advance triumphantly as a weaponless army of liberation behind Jesus, Lord of Hosts.

JESUS LIFTED UP TO HEAVEN

38. "From now on you will see the Son of Man seated at the right hand of the Power," Jesus had said at the climax of his trial. And now he approaches his rightful place, riding "on the heights of the ancient heavens" (Ps. 68:34).

> High above all nations is the LORD,
> above the heavens is his glory.
> Who is like the LORD, our God, who is enthroned on high
> and looks upon the heavens and the earth below?
> (Ps. 113:4–6)

It is because Jesus emptied himself, humbled himself even to death on a cross, that God has exalted him. And because he enters the heavenly sanctuary also as high priest, Jesus "might now appear before God on our behalf" (Heb. 9:24). He is a high priest who is "holy, innocent, undefiled, separated from sinners, higher than the heavens" (Heb. 7:26).

Brother, this is wonderful, but . . . it seems so *distant!*

Ah, be careful! In all this glory as Jesus ascends to the height of heaven, do not forget to be astonished that it is *the man* Jesus so ascending and so glorified. And while angels sang around him, Jesus entered the heavens *bodily*, bringing right before the face of God the stark humanness of scarred and wounded flesh.

Flesh.

Yes. Into this transformed heaven, our hearts and our bodies too are welcomed to join the angels in their praise of God.

JESUS ABUNDANTLY GIVING THE SPIRIT

Acts 2:1–4

39. In the instant of Jesus' ascension and enthronement—a time beyond the separation of moment from moment—time passed slowly as the disciples, still bewildered and anxious, gathered to prepare for the next surprise beyond anticipation. It was seven weeks from the Resurrection—a time of completion, a time of ripeness.

I remember the story. Suddenly a whirlwind embraced the place where they stayed, and the Spirit descended, reaching within each of them. These timid and uneducated people then burst boldly out of their place of hiding and spoke with inspiration to the citizens of the world who had gathered curiously outside. Suddenly insight flooded the disciples' minds with understanding of what Jesus had said and done while he was with them. Suddenly ardor and determination fired their hearts.

From that spark, like a brushfire, the good news spread throughout the known world by the effort and suffering of these weak men turned into firebrands. Communities of believers sprang up, so that the proclamation "Jesus Christ is Lord!" echoed from Alexandria to Philippi, from Jerusalem to Rome. In these Christian communities the Spirit enabled struggling people to overcome the inertia of vice and injustice, to open minds to surprise, to enlighten intellects to truth beyond understanding, and to begin gathering the harvest into oneness with God.

The harvest . . . the end of the world?

The *goal* of the world! As Jesus was enthroned in the renewal of heaven, the Spirit which he sent forth began the renewal and transformation of the earth. And the Church, like leaven, is the sign and the instrument of that transformation. Jesus looks upon the Church with love, making her holy and cleansing her so that he might present her to himself in splendor, without spot or wrinkle or any such thing, that she might be to him a bride holy and without blemish (see Eph. 5:25–27). And the wandering world has looked upon the Church with fear and astonishment:

> Who is this that comes forth like the dawn,
> as beautiful as the moon, as resplendent as the sun,
> as awe-inspiring as bannered troops?
> (Song of Songs 6:10)

So . . . the end of the world is happening *now?* I mean, the goal of the world is being accomplished *now?*

Yes. The coming of the Spirit has given a new beginning to history—overcoming the disintegration begun by Adam, and advancing the reconciliation begun by Christ. The gathering of disciples, the Church, is empowered by the Spirit to make this transformation happen—in each heart and in each community and even to the ends of the earth.

In each heart . . .

That is what is happening in your heart as well. Empowered by the Spirit, you are caught up beyond yourself in the power of God at work everywhere. The powerful *will to save* that led Jesus to suffer and die—that same powerful will is given to each of us:

> "The Spirit of the Lord is upon me
> because he has anointed me
> to bring glad tidings to the poor.
> He has sent me to proclaim liberty to captives
> and recovery of sight to the blind,
>   to let the oppressed go free.
> (Luke 4:18)

I feel that urgent warmth in my heart, Brother Bonaventure. As I look from these lofty branches over the wide, sad earth— So much must be done! So much healed! So much fostered, and so much forgiven! I groan within myself with longing for the completion of the Spirit's work!

Has your heart then become a bit like Jesus' own heart? Now that the "I" is no more, with its worries over status and personal salvation, have you been caught up in the living power of Christ?

Uh . . . honestly, I don't know!

No, you would not. But open your heart—the Spirit of Jesus will be at work in us beyond what we can know or say or do. Be careful to keep the "I" from reviving and getting in his way! It will! Like weeds! (That is why the Spirit brings, among other gifts, forgiveness and laughter.) Focus on Jesus and the mission he has given. As for yourself—why be distracted with worry over rubbish? Let yourself fly free in the whirlwind of the Spirit.

JESUS, THE CONDEMNED, SETS FREE

40. So Jesus ascends into his glory—he who was rejected, harassed, condemned and killed by complacent and self-protecting people. But do you notice something conspicuously absent from Jesus' songs of triumph?

I think so! Even Jeremiah, that suffering servant whose misery foreshadowed the path of Jesus, gave in to it:

> So now, deliver their children to famine,
> do away with them by the sword.
> Let their wives be made childless and widows;
> let their men die of pestilence,
> their young men be slain by the sword in battle... .
> For they have dug a pit to capture me,
> they have hid snares for my feet.
> (Jeremiah 18:21–22)

> Happy the man who shall seize and smash
> your little ones against the rock!
> (Ps. 137:9)

Jesus did not seek *vengeance.* A saving high priest rather than a vengeful warrior-king, Jesus established a saving order in the world by which the power of God would reach outward to every creature, and then draw all to return to unity, reconciling all things. The visible Church participates in this saving order as Jesus provides it with roles of service, charismatic gifts, and sacraments—all ordered to "building up the body of Christ, until we all attain to the unity of faith and knowledge of the Son of God . . . to the extent of the full stature of Christ" (Eph. 4:12–13). Jesus himself is the head of his body—the mystery of Church that is visible and that transcends the visible—and from him the whole body brings about its growth and builds itself up in love (Eph. 4:16).

History and my own life tell me that there are growing pains in the playing out of this saving order!

Of course! To grow to the full stature of Christ means to be crucified with him, doesn't it? Hadn't you noticed how well trodden is the path we have been following?

Well trodden? I felt so desperately alone, especially in the middle branches!

Poor silly fool! Of course, I had forgotten. Your heart was still blinded by the "I" and you couldn't see that you were together with Mary, with the apostles and martyrs, and with all the saints through-out the ages.

Now, conscious of our union with them, we praise God as Church. But why is there still the pain? Oh, I see: the saving order Jesus has established has yet to reach its completion.

Yes, and there is another dimension that Jesus' saving order embraces, not only Church and humankind. Creation itself awaits with eager expectation—it is groaning in labor pains even until now, and we groan with it (Rom. 8:19–23). We have to undo the old pattern of vengeance if creation is to be saved. Human beings have exploited and killed others for power or for gain—seeking status, security, and control over destiny. Trust in princes or in arms or in riches is merely the "I" asserting itself. Even with Adam, the "I" sought to make itself like God, and thereby slashed the gentle bonds that bind together the creatures of the earth. As a result the Tree of Life, that once ordered Paradise as its center, was lost. After that there were only self-destructive scramble and the disorder of exploitation and illusion.

The Tree of Life was lost ?

Yes, and yet we rest upon the Tree of Life. Now it is the center of Jesus' saving order. Not only are we set free from sin and guilt. Creation too is set free from the tyranny of "I" with its exploitation, waste and destruction.

Not so you'd notice! Have you any idea how the earth has been bruised, bled and drained in the centuries between us?

Yes. The power of "I" is still a long way from extinction! And yet, your age is more aware than I ever could be of how the earth is one. You can see more directly how all of its people are being reconciled by the anonymous workings of Christ's saving order. Does that urgent warmth still stir in your heart? Set it to work for the reconciliation of person with person, of humanity with earth. That is *your* serving role within the saving order that Jesus has established.

11

The Equity of His Judgment

The seed has been sown. Then comes the time of growth—a time of spreading of the good news, a time of transforming the earth like leaven, a time of the power of the Spirit at work bringing reconciliation. However, it is also the troubling time of weeds and wheat growing ambiguously together. It is the time of your serving role as well.

But the earth is so vast, and the challenge so overwhelming!

Have you learned nothing? Why are you terrified, O you of little faith? It is the power of Christ at work, not your own effort. If Christ could bring such triumph from a cross, imagine what he can do with us even in spite of our disasters! And so you set out in hope, doing the very best you can do, but knowing that what really matters is what God is doing—and we might not understand that! It will all come out only in the end, when all secrets are revealed, even God's.

The judgment! I had always been fearful of Judgment Day.

There is reason to fear if you think you must have achieved a perfection of righteousness. But that's the "I" again, fearing for its own security and desperate to control its destiny.

I wondered. That fear has evaporated, and I felt a twinge—is it *bad* that the fear evaporated? I guess it had really been drummed into me as a child. Now as I look ahead to that day I feel mostly . . . eagerness, almost curiosity. We will see the unfolding of the mystery, of God's secret plan for history, and we'll discover how we each fit into it and how we touched each other, for good or for ill. I expect surprises, sobering ones and joyful ones. I expect . . . well, there has to be forgiveness, and there has to be laughter.

There will be surprises. Are you ready?

JESUS, TRUTHFUL WITNESS

41. As we imagine the time of the future judgment, we picture the dead rising and all humankind from all ages gathering together before Jesus as judge:

> The LORD is King. . . .
> Clouds and darkness are round about him,
> justice and judgment are the foundation of his throne.
> Fire goes before him. . . .
> His lightnings illumine the world;
> the earth sees and trembles.
> (Ps. 97:1–4)

Have you harbored thoughts like "Then they'll get what's coming to them"? Watch out for surprises:

> Why then do you judge your brother? Or you, why do you look down on your brother? For we shall all stand before the judgment seat of God. . . . So [then] each of us shall give an account of himself [to God]. (Rom. 14:10, 12).

Delusions will be exposed and pretenses unmasked. The self-deception of the hypocrite will be shattered, and the hidden exploitation by the respectable indicted.

> "There is nothing concealed that will not be revealed, nor secret that will not be known. Therefore whatever you have said in the darkness will be heard in the light, and what you have whispered behind closed doors will be proclaimed on the housetops." (Luke 12:2–3).

That could prove very embarrassing!

It gives one a motive for keeping one's behavior impeccable, even when out of public scrutiny.

Brother Bonaventure, get serious! "If you, O LORD, mark iniquities, LORD, who can stand?" (Ps. 130:3).

You have a point, but at least we will all share the embarrassment! Then the wisdom of Jesus' words will be all too apparent: "Stop judging, that you may not be judged" (Matt. 7:1). Condemning evil is not the only thing that is done by the justice of God. For on that day his justice will be revealed beyond any conventional measure of good and evil—the justice of God that *justifies* by grace, through the redemption that is in Christ Jesus, to be received by faith (Rom. 3:21–25). Look at the next verse of that psalm you just quoted: "But with you is forgiveness, that you may be revered" (Ps. 130:4).

There has to be forgiveness. And then embarrassment will be transformed into laughter.

There will also be laughter of pure joy. Not all of the secrets revealed will be embarrassing ones. The beauty of a silent spiritual struggle will bring delight to all. The unseen effect of a kindness will be shown. The book of life will be opened fully. The whole of history that we have seen only moment by moment, stitch by stitch, will be raised up and displayed like a huge, awesome tapestry. The thread of each of our lives—with deeds so ambiguous and so confusing, so full of ups and downs, struggles and pains—that thread will shine forth in its place in the pattern, and we will rejoice in astonishment at its beauty.

> The one who judges me is the Lord. Therefore, do not make any judgment before the appointed time, until the Lord comes, for he will bring to light what is hidden in darkness and will manifest the motives of our hearts, and then everyone will receive praise from God. (1 Cor. 4:4–5).

Praise?
Praise.

JESUS, WRATHFUL JUDGE

Matthew 24–25
Mark 13
Luke 21

42. *Everyone* will receive praise from God? What about the wicked? The stories of the judgment tell of goats separated from sheep, of weeds separated from wheat and burnt in the fire. There is a hell, right?

Yes. What is your point?

Then not everyone will receive praise from God!

How do you know? Have you already been to the final judgment? Do you have census records from hell? These Gospel stories are not factual history written in advance. They are written to guide our hearts to true discipleship. The stories that tell of God's *praise* in judgment guide us to remember:

> As I live, says the LORD, I swear I take no pleasure in the death of the wicked man, but rather in the wicked man's conversion, that he may live. (Ezek. 33:11)

The stories that tell of God's *wrath* guide us to remember, "Whoever thinks he is standing secure should take care not to fall" (1 Cor. 10:12).

So . . . we don't *know* what will happen at the judgment.

Of course not! Be open to surprises! Imagine that gathering: righteous Pharisees next to sleazy tax collectors; impeccable priests next to gaudy prostitutes; respectable , law-abiding citizens next to bandits. And then the basis for judgment is revealed. What saves is not righteousness by the law, not attachment to the temple, not virtue. What condemns is not shady dealing, dirty sex, or outlawry. What saves is simple human kindness for others! What condemns is indifference to the sufferings of others!

What astonishment will rock the crowd. What an incredible surprise!

The Pharisee will protest, But Lord, what about my years of faithful prayer and works of virtue? He will reply, faithful? Real faith is not a matter of fulfilling obligations or self-consciously perform-ing pious works. Real faith naturally overflows into loving kindness (see Gal. 5:6). Look carefully: it's not only the obviously wicked that the Apocalypse shows hiding in caves from the wrath of God. "The kings of the earth, the nobles, the military officers, the rich, the powerful, and every slave and free person" scamper in terror (Rev. 6:15). That about covers the whole population, doesn't it? *Everybody* is in for surprises!

Who then can be saved?

Why are you terrified, O you of little faith? Your "I" is judged already. Let your heart pray,

> O LORD, hear my prayer;
>   hearken to my pleading in your faithfulness;
>   in your justice answer me.
> And enter not into judgment with your servant,
> for before you no living man is just.
> (Ps. 143:1–2).

JESUS, GLORIOUS CONQUEROR

43. As wrathful judgment is passed on the wicked, the universe is purged. The angel of everlasting good news announces to every nation, tribe, tongue and people, "Fear God and give him glory, for his time has come to sit in judgment" (Rev. 14:7). And all who worshiped the evil beast

> "will also drink the wine of God's fury, poured full strength into the cup of his wrath, and will be tormented in burning sulfur before the holy angels and before the Lamb. The smoke of the fire that torments them will rise forever and ever, and there will be no relief day or night for those who worship the beast." (Rev. 14:10–11).

The beast and his false prophet are thrown into the fiery pool burning with sulfur, and their followers are turned into carrion (c.f. Rev. 19:20–21).

Um . . . Brother Bonaventure, something bothers me about this.
Really!

I mean, when we saw Jesus ascend into his glory, wasn't this spirit
of vengeance conspicuously absent? And instead of pitting good
against evil as if the universe were ultimately and hopelessly split,
wasn't Jesus' saving order supposed to bring reconciliation of all
humankind, even of the earth and the whole physical universe? If
so many are cast into an everlasting stinkpot and if the whole earth
is crunched up like an old paper cup—hasn't Jesus *failed?*

That question *should* bother you.

Well, which is it? Is the last word apocalyptic destruction or
universal reconciliation?

Yes.

Huh?

How are we to know? Have you already been to the final judgment and heard the last word? Again, these stories are not history
written in advance, but they are given to guide our hearts to true
discipleship. If the last word is only the reconciliation of all, then
what is the point of struggling toward good and fighting against
evil? If the last word is apocalyptic division and destruction, then
what is the point of hoping for forgiveness and of valuing the earth
and its peoples? What is the point of Christ's death *for sinners?*
Either word without the other is false; each word is true only in
relation to the other.

Once again, there will be surprises!

Be wary, for traps are set here for those whose life is centered on
"I". Some are rendered complacent, insensible, by a presumptuous
expectation of universal reconciliation. But the traps are far more
dangerous to those who seize upon the apocalyptic vision. These
people divide the earth into the few good (themselves included,
of course) and the evil empire of Antichrist, which they identify
as everything that challenges the puny "I" that they jealously
protect. The presumption of the first group is soft and amiable;
the presumption of these is unforgiving and humorless, sharp
and vicious.

Oh, my Brother, I can hear again those horrible shouts in Pilate's
courtyard. "Away with him! Away with him! Crucify him! And all
will be well . . ." Those caught in the apocalyptic trap echo that
shout—and their presumption leads them to hate others, perhaps
just because they are different. It leads them to *kill*—sometimes to
kill thousands upon thousands of innocent people. All in the name
of the battle of the righteous against Antichrist!

The most bitter irony is that by so doing, these very people have worshiped that vicious parody of the Lamb that was slain. These people have *become* the Antichrist they so zealously battle! These are the most difficult to waken from their delusion—and they hang only by a slender thread over the fiery pit. How vicious are the claims of the "I" that pursues guarantees for its own security, certitude and salvation!

JESUS, ADORNED SPOUSE

44. When in the equity of his judgment Jesus has subjected everything to himself (see 1 Cor. 15:23–28), "I also saw the holy city, a new Jerusalem, coming down out of heaven from God, prepared as a bride adorned for her husband" (Rev. 21:2).

> Then I heard something like the sound of a great multitude or the sound of rushing water or mighty peals of thunder, as they said:
>
>> "Alleluia!
>> The Lord has established his reign. . . .
>> Let us rejoice and be glad
>> and give him glory.
>> For the wedding day of the Lamb has come,
>> his bride has made herself ready.
>> (Rev. 19:6–7).

The Church, in its full mystery as the body of Christ, is now purified and ready for the wedding feast. Now this great multitude, which no one could count, from every nation, race, people and tongue (Rev. 6:9), is clothed in the white robe of incorruptibility and immortality (see 1 Cor. 15:53).

Even here at the heavenly wedding feast there are surprises, aren't there? For the invited ones, those who were convinced of their own worthiness, have become entangled in the concerns of "I." And in their place, full of astonishment, come the poor and the crippled, the blind and the lame (see Luke 17:9, 14:15–24).

> Who is like the LORD, our God, who is enthroned on high
> and looks upon the heavens and the earth below?
> He raises up the lowly from the dust;
> from the dunghill he lifts up the poor.
> (Ps. 113:5–7)

Those who are ready—who have let go of claims of the "I" and have kept their lamps lit with a hope beyond expectations—enter the wedding feast of the kingdom of heaven.

Justice will bring about peace;
right will produce calm and security.
My people will live in peaceful country,
in secure dwellings and quiet resting places.
(Isa. 32:17–18)

12

The Eternity of His Kingdom

Now we come to rest on the last of the lofty branches of the Tree of Life, those that bear the leaves and fruits of Jesus' coming into his glory.

Look! We can see more than the expanse of the earth and the height of the heavens from here, Brother Bonaventure. We can see all of history coming to its completion in the fullness of time. We can see our own times in relation to that completion. We can see the unfolding of Christ's kingdom in heaven and on earth!

Yes, we can see—but indistinctly, through the mirror of story and symbol. We can know—but partially, through meditation and reflection. We are not yet in the final kingdom, you know. Even when we are crucified with Christ, and when we have touched every leaf and tasted every fruit of the Tree of Life, we are still upon the earth and in time.

I recognize that Christ's kingdom is to be prayed for and hoped for—"Thy kingdom come!"

Recognize another thing. While we rest on these branches, just as Moses stood on holy ground on the mountain of God, be ready to hear what he heard. Yes, God is doing wonderful works to bring his people into the promised kingdom. But how is he accomplishing that? "Come now! I will send *you* . . ." (see Exod. 3:4–10).

I remember. "Thy will be done!" That means doing.

JESUS, KING, SON OF THE KING

45. "He has a name written on his cloak and on his thigh, 'King of kings and Lord of lords' " (Rev. 19:16). Jesus is King subjecting everything to himself— over all the powers of heaven and earth. Yet as King, he is Son:

> When everything is subjected to him, then the Son himself will be subjected to the one who subjected everything to him, so that God may be all in all. (1 Cor. 15:28)

So it shall be when Jesus brings to fullness the everlasting power of his kingdom. His reign will be governed by the power of truth, love and peace. All differences will be reconciled without becoming homogeneous, and all diversities will become one while losing nothing of their uniqueness. In this kingdom, the more one gives of one's heart, the more one's heart is truly itself. The vaster the multitudes of this kingdom, the more familial are the ties binding all together. "And they shall reign forever and ever" (Rev. 22:5).

Brother Bonaventure, this vision tells of more than the final kingdom, doesn't it?

Of course! We can hear it telling also of earth and of the inner life of God.

I see how it tells of earth and of our own time. The qualities of the final kingdom are truth, love and peace; relationships in the kingdom are marked by selfless sharing, reconciliation of the opposed, and communion among the diverse. Those qualities are present in our own world and times—present, but obscured and hindered. If we have been sent forth to work toward the kingdom, then it is our task to foster such qualities and such relationships. If God's will is to be done on earth, then our task is to overcome obstacles and hindrances to the coming of the kingdom. If indeed the kingdom means renewal of the heavens and the earth, it is our task to reverse the harm done to the earth and the heavens.

Yes. For that God sends you as he sent Moses, and as he sent Jesus! And yet there is an even more powerful insight here. These tasks are too great for us! Yet we are called to bring them about. The *power* of the kingdom catches us up and empowers us—power that emerges from the Father as Origin. It is manifest in Jesus the Son and in the multitude who follow him. Finally it is fulfilled when all are led back by the power of the Spirit to the unity of the Father—so that God may be all in all.

In mounting the Tree of Life, then, not only are we being crucified with Christ . . .

. . . we are being caught up into the dynamic life of God and into God's work in history: "In the name of the Father, and of the Son, and of the holy Spirit" (Matt. 28:19).

JESUS, INSCRIBED BOOK

46. This kingdom is governed by Wisdom. Jesus is himself the book of life, the Word, written in wisdom by the Father. What an incomparable book! If only we can find it!

> For he who finds me finds life,
> and wins favor from the LORD;
> But he who misses me harms himself;
> all who hate me love death.
> (Prov. 8:35–36)

Brother Bonaventure, why do you say the book is so hard to find? Aren't you speaking of the Bible?

The Bible? That is only the most external expression of this book. After all, we have been praying the Bible in our ascent of the Tree of Life, and we have yet really to find this book. The Bible does tell of it, though, and through the Bible one might be led toward finding it.

Then what is this book, and where shall we search for it?

This book is first the Uncreated Word, whose origin is eternal and whose essence is incorruptible.

> The LORD begot me, the firstborn of his ways,
> the forerunner of prodigies of long ago;
> From of old I was poured forth,
> at the first, before the earth. . . .
> When he established the heavens I was there, . . .
> when he fixed fast the foundations of the earth; . . .
> Then was I beside him as his craftsman,
> and I was his delight day by day.
> (Prov. 8:22–23, 27–28, 30)

This volume is the book of creation, which expresses the limitless fullness of the creative power of the Father. To read this book, recognize in every creature the power and wisdom of God, and be led back through creatures to his goodness in praise. This book's teaching is easy, but those who find it are few.

And that is only one aspect of this book . . .

This book next is the Inspired Word, whose script is indelible and whose knowledge is life.

> If you seek her like silver,
> and like hidden treasures search her out:
> Then will you understand the fear of the LORD;
> the knowledge of God you will find;
> For the LORD gives wisdom,
> from his mouth come knowledge and understanding.
> (Prov. 2:4–6)

This volume of the book is the enlightenment which inflames the minds of the heavenly citizens, when all is revealed.

Is there even more?

Yes: finally, this book is the Incarnate Word, who came into flesh, lived upon the earth, and revealed his glory. The Gospels tell of this Word. And yet, "This saying is hard; who can accept it?" (John 6:60). For all humankind the study of this volume of the book is desirable. But "no one can come to me unless it is granted him by my Father" (John 6:65), for the depth of this book is inscrutable and its words are ineffable. Therefore the Incarnate Word comes also as a gift into our hearts, and when that happens the knowledge of the book is sweet.

> With that their eyes were opened and they recognized him. . . . Then they said to each other, "Were not our hearts burning [within us] while he spoke to us on the way and opened the scriptures to us? (Luke 24:31–32)

All these books are but one Word: Jesus, Word of the Father, the book written within and without. One does not take up this book; one is taken up by it, gathered into it. Again, we are swept up into the saving life of God: the Father speaks forth the Word of revealing wisdom, and the Spirit leads all back to the knowledge of God.

Then . . . God's *revelation* is not merely a bound book one holds in one's hands. Nor is it merely a content of knowledge, a set of doctrines or stories. What is it?

Revelation *happens* when the Word Incarnate comes into the heart. To read this Word is to go beyond words, and to be struck dumb in astonishment and joy. Revelation may happen in beauty as we open our hearts to the world around us. Revelation may happen in truth as we open our hearts to the hearts of others. Revelation may happen in goodness as we open our hearts to the mystery of God's will.

But . . . none of this is particularly *new*. The world has been around us all along, and others too—and the mystery of God's will has been at work all along.

Of course! When all things are made new, all things remain. The revelation happens when finally, as for the first time, we see and appreciate them for what they really are.

It is like the husband and wife looking back over years of struggle and uncertainty and disappointment, and finally seeing—yes, this is really our life, and in spite of everything it is beautiful and true and good.

> O my dove in the clefts of the rock,
> in the secret recesses of the cliff,
> Let me see you,
> let me hear your voice,

For your voice is sweet,
and you are lovely.
(Song of Songs 2:14)

JESUS, FOUNTAIN-RAY OF LIGHT

47. The source and goal of the kingdom is the goodness of God. This goodness is like a fountain flowing into rivers of life-giving water over all the earth. This goodness is like the fiery light of the sun, radiating outward over the entire universe. Jesus, light from light, is the flowing river of God's goodness, the pure ray of God's light.

"Let anyone who thirsts come to me and drink.
Whoever believes in me, as scripture says:
'Rivers of living water will flow from within him.' "
(John 7:37–38)
"Whoever drinks the water I shall give will never thirst;
the water I shall give will become in him
a spring of water welling up to eternal life."
(John 4:14)

This infinite, overflowing goodness and this inaccessible, emanating light—which has given rise even to the sun and other stars—reach and radiate through Jesus toward *us*. It is so generously close, and our hearts rise in grateful astonishment.

I . . . is it all right to reach out and . . .

Yes! Touch and be touched by the overflowing goodness of God. Drink freely of the love of God.

There is a stream whose runlets gladden the city of God,
the holy dwelling of the Most High.
(Ps. 46:5)

Deep calls unto deep
in the roar of your cataracts;
All your breakers and your billows
pass over me.
(Ps. 42:8)
O LORD, your kindness reaches to heaven;
your faithfulness, to the clouds. . . .
From your delightful stream you give them to drink.
For with you is the fountain of life,
and in your light we see light.
(Ps. 36:6, 9–10).

I realize something now, Brother. When my feet were flung from footing and my hands torn from clinging, I spun into a terrifying fall. But all at once the terror left, darkness became light, and falling became like flying. But what happened was . . . my heart was being caught up in the bright current of the goodness of God! My heart was floating in the river of the goodness of God!

You are just realizing that now? Don't you see that every being *exists* only by floating in this current that comes forth from God through the Word and returns to God by the power of the Spirit? But now that you realize what has always been so real, you receive a twofold task. One is to look to the source that gives forth this radiating stream, and to rejoice and be nourished in it. The other is to look downstream:

> "Have you seen this, son of man?" Then he brought me to the bank of the river. He said to me, "This water flows into the sea, which it makes fresh. Wherever the river flows, every sort of creature shall live. Along both banks of the river fruit trees of every kind shall grow; their leaves shall not fade, nor their fruit fail. Their fruit shall serve for food, and their leaves for medicine." (from Ezek. 47:6–12).

The Tree of Life!

Like the Tree of Life, you are nourished by the river that flows forth from the throne of God and of the Lamb. If the "I" is no more, then your leaves will not fade from discouragement, nor your fruit fail from obstacles or hindrances. You are sent forth to nourish and heal wherever you go.

The Tree of Life is . . . in *us?*

If you have been crucified with Christ . . .

Then "insofar as I now live in the flesh, I live by faith in the Son of God who has loved me and given himself up for me" (Gal. 2:20).

And consciously or unconsciously it is his work you do wherever you go, by the power of the Spirit.

> Come! Behold the deeds of the LORD,
>   the astounding things he has wrought on earth.
> (Ps. 46:9)

JESUS, DESIRED GOAL

48. Tell me, why did you undertake this climbing of the Tree of Life?

What? Oh . . . Gee, let me think! Oh, that's right. I desired to worship God and to be a disciple of Christ.

Why?

What do you mean, why! I guess . . . I remember that deep longing in my heart. I guess I desired happiness.

What is happiness?

Come now, Brother Bonaventure! Who can define such a word as "happiness" or "blessedness"?

One of my favorite philosophers defines it as "a state of being which is made perfect by the gathering together of all goods." What do you think of that?

How can *all* goods be together at once? Tell your philosopher friend that he makes happiness impossible!

Really? Look more closely at this last healing leaf around the fruit of Jesus' glory.

> "I am the Alpha and the Omega," says the Lord God, "the one who is and who was and who is to come." (Rev. 1:8)

In himself Jesus gathers beginning and end; past, present and future all at once.

> He is the image of the invisible God,
> the firstborn of all creation.
> For in him were created all things in heaven and on earth,
> the visible and the invisible;
> all things were created through him and for him.
> He is before all things,
> and in him all things hold together.
> He is the head of the body, the church.
> He is the beginning, the firstborn from the dead,
> that in everything he might be preeminent.
> For in him all the fulness of God was pleased to dwell,
> and through him to reconcile to himself all things,
> whether on earth or in heaven,
> making peace by the blood of his cross.
> (from Col. 1:15–20, RSV)

So Jesus himself *is* a state of being which is made perfect by the gathering together of all goods! As Word he is origin of everything; in his crucified flesh he restores everything and brings everything to completion; and he indeed *is* that completion and goal of all things.

So in Jesus is happiness. Of course! But . . . frankly, Brother Bonaventure, my own happiness seems now like a really trivial concern! We have been caught up into currents that are so powerful, and so demanding!

That is the beautiful irony of the Tree of Life! Happiness is never attained by a purposeful "I" striving for it.

"If anyone wishes to come after me, he must deny himself and take up his cross. . . . For whoever wishes to save his life will lose it, but whoever loses his life for my sake will save it." (Luke 9:23–24)

When you began this ascent, you were driven by longing and drawn by desire for happiness. But as you progressed, the "I" that is at the root of desire fell away and the longing in your heart became one with the groaning of all creation for the completion of Jesus' mission. And now you are among the loftiest branches of the Tree of Life. Your desire for happiness has become irrelevant because there is no more "I." But the life in your heart is following the way of complete return to oneness with Jesus.

I can only hope that that is really happening!

Hope . . . and pray. But rise, and have no fear. Remember who it is that makes it happen!

"Behold, I am coming soon. . . . I am the Alpha and the Omega, the first and the last, the beginning and the end." (Rev. 22:12, 13)

Happy are they who may come to the Tree of Life.

PRAYER FOR THE GIFTS OF THE SPIRIT

49. Oh, Brother Bonaventure, for all our climbing together and our struggle and our anguish—I am only at the beginning! God only knows if all this is real within my heart!

Yes, I'm sure God does know! But we do not, nor can we. Nor should we! We are a joke that amuses God, for the "I" keeps popping up like a weed, popping out like a slip-hem or a shirttail. Therefore, pray to the Father through Jesus: May the Spirit be at work in us even in spite of ourselves.

> The spirit of the LORD shall rest upon him:
> a spirit of wisdom and understanding,
> A spirit of counsel and of strength,
> a spirit of knowledge and of fear of the LORD,
> and his delight shall be the fear of the LORD.
> (Isa. 11:2–3)

By wisdom we taste the fruit of the Tree of Life that is Jesus. By understanding our minds and hearts are enlightened in the mysteries of Jesus' origin, passion and glory. By counsel we are guided to make choices that follow Jesus' way. By strength we persevere in spite of failure and we prevail in spite of weakness. By knowledge the Good News enters and enlightens our hearts to dispel delusion and cling to the true. By piety all our relationships are touched with patience and loving kindness. By the fear of the Lord we recognize who God is, and we stand in awe—realizing that nothing really matters but God.

Nothing really matters but God. And everything matters only in God, who is all in all.

And now, Father, we ask that you transform our heart by these gifts. Make it happen in us that "I have been crucified with Christ; yet I live, no longer I, but Christ lives in me" (Gal. 2:19–20). Let us be caught up in the mystery of your will, in your plan for the fullness of time, so that through us, too, Jesus reconciles to himself all things, whether on earth or in heaven, making peace by the blood of his cross.

Oh, the depth of the riches and wisdom and knowledge of God!
How inscrutable are his judgments and how unsearchable his ways!

"For who has known the mind of the Lord
or who has been his counselor?
Or who has given him anything
that he may be repaid?"
For from him and through him and for him are all things. To him be glory forever. Amen. (Rom. 11:33–36)

Here Ends the Tree of Life

Notes

The Soul's Journey into God

Prologue

1. Bonaventure, *The Soul's Journey into God; The Tree of Life; The Life of St. Francis*, trans. Ewert H. Cousins (New York: Paulist Press, 1978). All English language quotations from St. Bonaventure are taken from this translation.

2. *Regula Bullata*, chapter 10, *Francis and Clare, The Complete Works*, trans. Regis Armstrong and Ignatius Brady (New York: Paulist Press, 1982), p. 144.

Chapter 2. Body

1. A useful set of exercises to awaken bodily awareness for Christian spiritual growth has been developed by Anthony de Mello in *Sadhana: A Way to God; Christian Exercises in Eastern Form* (Garden City, NY: Image Books, 1984).

2. *The Poems of Gerard Manley Hopkins*, 4th ed. (New York: Oxford University Press, 1967), #38.

3. Augustine, *Confessions*, trans. John K. Ryan (Garden City, NY: Image Books, 1960), Book I c. 1; p. 43.

Chapter 3. Thought and Action

1. See Augustine, *De Trinitate*, Book XIV, c. 12, n. 15; *Confessiones*, Book I, c.1.

2. For Bonaventure's understanding of the relationship of academic disciplines to each other, see *De Reductione Artium ad Theologiam, Opera Omnia*, V, 317–325; for his condemnation of narrow specialization, see especially *Collationes in Hexaemeron*, I:17, V, 332.

Chapter 4. Grace

1. Dante, *The Divine Comedy: Paradiso*, trans. Dorothy L. Sayers (New York: Penguin, 1962), XXXIII:145.

Chapter 5. The One God

1. See M. Lucy del Mastro, "Walter Hilton's *Scala Perfectionis*: A

Circular Stairway," in *Itinerarium: The Idea of Journey*, ed. Leonard J. Bowman (Salzburg: 1983), pp. 178–201.

2. *Poems of Gerard Manley Hopkins*, #155.

3. See Nicholas of Cusa, *De Docta Ignorantia*, Book I, c. 13–15.

4. Quoting Alan of Lille, *Regulae Theologicae*, reg. 7.

Chapter 7. Rest

1. Arnaldo Fortini, *Francis of Assisi*, trans. Helen Moak (New York: Crossroad, 1980), p. 556.

2. Gregory of Nyssa, *The Life of Moses*, trans. Everett Ferguson and Abraham J. Malherbe (New York: Paulist Press, 1978), p. 113.

3. Ibid., p. 115.

4. Bonaventure here quotes Dionysius, *De mystica theologia*, I, 1.

Chapter 8. Back to Earth

1. Bonaventure, *Life of Frances*, 14:1, in Cousins, p. 315.

2. Lao Tzu, *Tao te Ching*, trans. Stephen Mitchell (New York: HarperCollins, 1991), 78.

3. *The Constitution of the Church in the Modern World*, Article 39, in *The Documents of Vatican II*, ed. Walter M. Abbott (New York: America Press, 1966).

The Tree of Life

Chapter 1. Hidden Brilliance in Jesus' Beginnings

1. In these reflections I have been guided by insights from Wilfred Cantwell Smith, particularly his *Faith and Belief* (Princeton, NJ: Princeton University Press, 1979), c. 5–6.

2. The Great "O" Antiphon for December 17th, translated from the *Liber Usualis* by the author.